PRAISE FOR *CHASING FAILURE*

"I've encouraged leaders for decades now to fail early, fail often, and to make sure you always fail forward. And what I love about Ryan's book and story is he has found a way to make failure enticing enough to make people take steps they'd never dream of taking. The principles and values outlined in this book are essential for a leader to grasp."

—John C. Maxwell
Author, speaker, and leadership expert

"*Chasing Failure* lends its readers a perspective that allows them to see the obstacles in their story as opportunities to grow. Ryan Leak continues to figure out ways to help people win when they feel like they're losing."

—Sam Collier
Lead Pastor of Hillsong Atlanta

"One of the most powerful things we can give the next generation is believing in them even after they've failed because belief is what helps them get back on their feet again. It's imperative for every parent, educator, coach, youth worker, and youth pastor to read *Chasing Failure* because students need Ryan's positive perspective, especially when they're experiencing setbacks."

—Tim Somers
Youth Pastor at Elevation Church

"Failure is inevitable in life. Learning from those failures is vital to your success. Ryan's book embodies that message, and it's one many more need to hear."

—Kevin Paul Scott
Speaker and author of *The Lens: Nine Shifts in a Leader's Perspective*

CHASING
FAILURE

CHASING FAILURE

HOW FALLING SHORT SETS YOU UP FOR SUCCESS

RYAN LEAK

W PUBLISHING GROUP

An Imprint of Thomas Nelson

Published in Nashville, Tennessee, by W Publishing, an imprint of Thomas Nelson.

Author is represented by the literary agency of The Fedd Agency, Inc., P. O. Box 341973, Austin, Texas, 78734.

Thomas Nelson titles may be purchased in bulk for educational, business, fund-raising, or sales promotional use. For information, please email SpecialMarkets@ThomasNelson.com.

Library of Congress Control Number: 2021904666

ISBN 978-0-7852-6160-5 (hardcover)
ISBN 978-0-7852-4089-1 (eBook)

Printed in the United States of America

21 22 23 24 25 LSC 10 9 8 7 6 5 4 3 2

To my beautiful wife, Amanda, I dedicate this book to you. It's difficult for any person with a dream to accomplish much without someone in their corner to believe they can touch the sky. I feel like the luckiest man in the world because you've been that for me since we first met. I told you about a dream on our first date and told you how scared I was. You responded, "It's not scary. It's fun." You changed my mind about going for the impossible, and because of you, I've been having fun facing my fears.

CONTENTS

FOREWORD

Almost everyone knows that Michael Jordan was cut from his high school basketball team. But most don't know that Walt Disney was once fired from a newspaper for a lack of ideas, and his first cartoon production company went bankrupt. Everyone loves Lucy, but Lucille Ball was told that she had no talent and should leave Murray Anderson's drama school. With all of Dustin Hoffman's success, it's hard to believe he worked as a janitor and an attendant in a psychiatric ward because he failed in his first attempt as an actor in New York.

Can you imagine Bob Dylan getting booed off the stage at his high school talent show? It's also hard to fathom Steven Spielberg not getting accepted to UCLA film school because of average grades. And it's easy to forget that Steve Jobs was fired from Apple at thirty years old and Oprah Winfrey was once told she wasn't fit for television and was fired as a news anchor.

The fact is, everyone fails in life, but it is a gift if you don't give up and are willing to learn, improve, and grow because of it.

Failure often serves as a defining moment, a crossroad on the journey of your life. It gives you a test designed to measure your courage, perseverance, commitment, and dedication. Are you a pretender who gives up after a little adversity . . . or a contender who keeps getting up after getting knocked down?

Failure provides you with a great opportunity to decide how much you really want something. Will you give up? Or will you dig deeper, commit more, work harder, learn, and get better? If you know that this is what you truly want, you will be willing to pay the price that greatness requires. You will be willing to fail again and again in order to succeed.

On the other hand, sometimes failure causes you take a different path that is better for you in the long run. When I lost my race for city council of Atlanta at the age of twenty-six, I realized that politics and all its negativity wasn't for me. This set me on a new course and ultimately led me to move my family to Florida and find my purpose of speaking and writing (now with more than twenty-three books published, with multiple bestsellers impacting millions of people around the globe).

Sometimes we have to lose a goal to find our destiny. Sometimes a failure helps us see what we really don't want and that we want something else.

Whatever path failure guides you toward, it is always meant to give you a big serving of humble pie that builds your character, gives you perspective, grows your faith, and makes you appreciate your success later on.

If you didn't fail, you wouldn't become the kind of person who ultimately succeeds.

And that's exactly what Ryan Leak shows you in *Chasing Failure*: how to embrace failure, use it, and make it your friend instead of your foe.

The next time you fail, don't let it keep you from the life you were born to live and the future you were meant to create. See failure as a test, a teacher, a detour to a better outcome and an event that builds a better you.

Failure is not meant to be final and fatal. It is not meant to define you. It is meant to refine you to be all that you are meant to be.

When you see failure as a blessing instead of a curse, you will turn the gift of failure into a stepping-stone that leads to the gift of success.

—Jon Gordon, 10-time bestselling author of *The Energy Bus* and *The Power of Positive Leadership*

ONE

SETTING YOU UP TO FAIL

You don't have to be great to get started, but
you do have to get started to be great.

—DENZEL WASHINGTON

What do you want to be when you grow up?

That's the question we're all presented with at
our adolescent stage where we feel like there's no real
wrong answer. Because when we're children, the possibilities are endless. When I was young, I wanted to be
in the NBA when I grew up. Specifically, I wanted to be
like Mike. I'd watch Michael Jordan on TV and then go
outside and pretend to be him, even in the rain.

"5 . . . 4 . . . 3 . . . 2 . . . 1 . . ."

As time expired, I would hit the game-winning shot with my tongue sticking out, and the crowd would go wild. In my mind, I was playing on the hardwood at the United Center in Chi-town, with thousands of people behind the backboard screaming my name; but in all reality, I was playing in front of my garage on the concrete pavement in my driveway.

Nobody ever told me I couldn't be like Mike. In fact, in middle school, my entire class was asked to put together a project outlining who we wanted to be when we grew up. That's when I detailed my entire NBA plan, beginning with going to the University of North Carolina and studying architecture. (I had a friend whose dad was an architect, and they were stupid rich. So I figured, why not have a nice fallback plan in case the whole NBA thing doesn't work out?) After four years at UNC, I would then be drafted by the Chicago Bulls, become a multimillionaire, and live happily ever after. It was that simple.

That's probably how it was for all of us as teenagers. We could all walk into our classrooms with hopes and dreams of becoming doctors, lawyers, politicians, astronauts, scientists, authors, professional athletes, singer-songwriters, filmmakers, and business moguls, with little to no resistance from outside sources. Many told us to dream big, but few admitted that we could fail.

It's easier to dream big when we're young because our failure awareness is rather low before we allow limitations to hold us back. I've found this to be especially true recently, because my son currently lives with a plethora of career options, including becoming an astronaut, a police officer, a firefighter, Captain America, and Black Panther. I told him it would be a good idea to just pick one job, and he said, "You have multiple jobs. So why can't I have multiple jobs?" Touché, Jaxson. Touché.

MANY TOLD US TO DREAM BIG, BUT FEW ADMITTED THAT WE COULD FAIL.

Kids can dream uninterrupted because failure has not yet become something they fear. Perhaps some parts of us should never grow up. Because as we grow up, failure becomes this invisible force that keeps us from doing the things we once dreamed of accomplishing. Our minds fill with excuses every time an opportunity to pursue a dream comes our way. And before we know it, we find ourselves settling for what we have to do instead of what we get to do. We move from dreaming as children to surviving as adults. I guess it's easier to dream when you have no bills.

Responsibilities and adulting often lead us to

IF WE'RE HONEST, THE BIGGEST REASON WE DON'T PURSUE OUR DREAMS IS BECAUSE THE DISTANCE BETWEEN OUR DREAMS AND OUR REALITIES IS OFTEN INTIMIDATING.

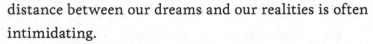

acquiesce to the status quo with little margin to think outside the box. We give ourselves full permission to accommodate average living because it's safer than taking a risk on something that could fail. Most of our dreams rarely come with health insurance.

If we're honest, the biggest reason we don't pursue our dreams is because the distance between our dreams and our realities is often intimidating.

Intimidation thoughts often sound like this:

What if it's not good?
What if nobody likes it?
Who do you think you are, trying to do that?
I don't have a degree for that.
I don't have the money to start that.
I don't know how websites work.
What's email marketing?
I don't have Facebook.
Oh, if we didn't have kids now, I would totally _____.

Here's what I know about you and me: we have mastered the art of talking ourselves out of being brave. We all do this because we'd rather tell ourselves that we're not good enough to do what we dream of doing before somebody else does. But that's a horrible way to live. Something magical could happen when you stop being afraid to be critiqued. We should never miss out on the life we dream of having because of what others might say about the dream.

The reality for you is that you're going to spend the next five years of your life doing something, whether it's average or extraordinary. Why not make the next five years the best years of your life and go for it? Why not spend the next five years actually taking steps in a direction you've daydreamed about?

Let me ask you a question that could absolutely change your life. It's the question that, for a moment, allows us to be a kid again:

What would you do if you knew you couldn't fail?

If you could remove failure from the equation and you knew success was a guarantee, what would you do? Would you write a book? Build an app? Open up your own restaurant? Produce music? Kick off your own fashion line? Start

WHAT WOULD YOU DO IF YOU KNEW YOU COULDN'T FAIL?

your own YouTube channel? Create your own podcast? Film a documentary? Fly planes? Set up a nonprofit organization? What's your idea that you would love to go for if you knew it was going to succeed?

In my twenties, my answer to this question was I would be in the NBA. So when I was twenty-eight, I decided to take my dream seriously. I began training for it and decided I was going to try to make it happen. Partway through my training, I had the opportunity to compete against a few former NBA players. I quickly realized I was headed on a one-way flight toward failure. So I decided to abort pursuing that dream.

Then I thought, *Why?* At previous times in my life, I had talked myself out of way too many ideas when I felt failure looming, but this time needed to be different. So I decided I was going to pursue my dream of playing in the NBA anyway.

Here's how I see it: we've got a long line of people in our world trying to chase success. But in all reality, every successful person you follow, look up to, or admire has one thing in common: *failures*. And yet, each and every one of them became the successful people they are, not in spite of, but *because* of those misfires, flops, and failures. So what makes the rest of us dare to think that we should run from the very things that made them who they are?

I started to wonder, *What if chasing failure was actually the quickest way to succeed?* So instead of getting in line to chase success, I decided to start a line for the brave who were willing to chase failure.

What's worse: failing while trying or failing by *not* trying? Even if I was just chasing failure by pursuing a chance to play in the NBA, at least I was taking action. I think you'll find you'll achieve a lot more by chasing failure rather than chasing success.

We all have something we'd love to do, but fear of failure often keeps us from moving toward who we could become. This becomes a self-fulfilling prophecy as we avoid going after things wholeheartedly, ultimately leading to failure by default. You've probably heard the phrase "Failure leads to success" a hundred times or more, but have you ever truly believed it? Have you ever actually put it to the test?

Po Bronson and Ashley Merryman's book *Top Dog: The Science of Winning and Losing* has profound insights and data on the stresses that come with competing and attempting things we could fail. One story from the book that stood out to me was about how researcher Renate Deinzer had people jump out of an airplane over and over to determine how their bodies responded to fear. She found that with each jump the amount of stress, though still large, decreased noticeably. By the third jump, she equated the level of stress to be on par with the same amount of stress someone would have running late to work.[1]

Over the next eleven chapters, I'm going to attempt to get you to jump out of the airplane. And I believe you'll be surprised what you can pull off when you're willing to keep jumping. By the end of our journey together, I hope failure loses its grip on your dreams. I want to help you reframe failure and remove the excuses you've given yourself for not even trying. This book isn't about trying to fail; it's about being willing to fail as you go after your dreams. It's about not being defeated by failure but rather learning all the lessons we can from it so we can be successful. If you find a gap between what you're doing in your life right now and what you would be doing if you knew you couldn't fail, this book is going to help you have the courage to take the next step. Maybe even the next two steps.

IF YOU FIND A GAP BETWEEN WHAT YOU'RE DOING IN YOUR LIFE RIGHT NOW AND WHAT YOU WOULD BE DOING IF YOU KNEW YOU COULDN'T FAIL, THIS BOOK IS GOING TO HELP YOU HAVE THE COURAGE TO TAKE THE NEXT STEP.

I'm not trying to convince you to quit your job or move to another country or sell all your possessions. I'm trying to help you level up from where you currently are so that you can be incredibly successful at achieving your dreams in a practical and realistic way. And yes, you might fail. And that's good news for you, because if you do, you'll join a club of the most successful people in the world. When we chase failure, with the goal of growing and striving for making our wildest dreams even an inkling more of a reality, then we are living a life that is not only successful but inspirational.

In this book, I am going to lay out the framework you need to chase failure successfully, which means living a life where you are pursuing your dreams, living in your purpose, and experiencing the most fulfillment possible. The framework will help you know whether or not your dream is one you need to be chasing. Then I will go over the game plan you need to implement in order to chase failure successfully and keep dreaming bigger to live your best life.

In a world obsessed with chasing success, I want to inspire and equip you to embrace the thing we've been taught to fear by chasing failure.

Am I setting you up to fail? I certainly hope so.

KEY TAKEAWAY

The distance between our dreams and realities is often intimidating. For us to put ourselves in a position to close the gap between where we are and where we want to go, we should start by answering this question: What would you do if you knew you couldn't fail?

TWO

KOBE MADE ME DO IT

Everything negative—pressure, challenges—
is all an opportunity for me to rise.

—KOBE BRYANT

How do you impress Kobe Bryant? This was the question I asked myself over and over before I met with my life-long hero in 2013 following a Lakers game.

Long story short: I proposed to my wife and surprised her with a wedding on the same day. We filmed the whole thing, and it went viral. (More on what became known as "The Surprise Wedding" in chapter 7.) One of the highlights of our fifteen minutes of fame was going on *The Queen Latifah Show*, where my wife surprised me with a video of Kobe Bryant inviting me to the Staples Center to meet him and the Lakers. I lost my mind but then gathered myself to get ready to meet a man I had admired for over a decade.

When preparing to meet one of the greatest basketball players of all time, I didn't want to be like every other fan he'd met. I didn't want an autograph (well, I did, but I had to play it cool, you know). I didn't want a photo to show to my friends. If I'm honest, I really wanted to make an impression on him because he had made one on me. I knew that he had met people from all over the world, so I wanted to have a conversation he would remember.

I figured the only way to get the attention of Mr. Bryant was to engage him in a conversation about a topic that was irresistible for him: *competition*. Whether Kobe was competing for the NBA Finals or a game of checkers, you'd get the same beast. I thought for us to have an engaging conversation, my attempting to work out with an NBA team would do the trick. (I imagined checkers wouldn't get his attention as effectively.)

I didn't just prepare to have a little meet-and-greet with Kobe. I prepared to play against Kobe if the opportunity presented itself. Before you laugh too hard, you should know I was an All-American at a small

Division III-ish college. (Our university's Division III status was pending when I played, and we were a part of the NCCAA, which stands for National Christian College Athletic Association. So among the Christian athletes in America . . . I was pretty good.) Nevertheless, I never pursued the pros. After training for a month or so, I played one-on-one against a friend who had just been cut from an NBA team. We played four or five games, and he won all of them by a fair margin. I remember thinking, *If he got cut from the league, then what on earth makes me think an NBA team would be interested in putting me on their roster?* I left the gym that day with the realization that if I tried out for an NBA team, I would most likely fail.

So I decided to give up on my dream. But then I realized I had never failed at becoming an NBA player before, so how could I know the outcome without even trying? And what's so scary about failing anyway? What's the worst that could happen if I tried and didn't make the cut? This was the day I decided to start chasing failure.

I began to envision a world where people weren't afraid to fail, and it was such an amazing picture that I had to find out for myself if failure, at the highest level, was really as bad as we all think. Most people entering into the NBA played Division I college or had

I HAD TO FIND OUT FOR MYSELF IF FAILURE, AT THE HIGHEST LEVEL, WAS REALLY AS BAD AS WE ALL THINK.

international professional experience. I had none of the above, but neither did Kobe—he entered the NBA straight out of high school.

When my wife and I arrived at Staples Center the night we were going to meet Kobe, the atmosphere was electric. A security guard came to our seats toward the end of the fourth quarter and led us to a private room in the back of the arena. I thought there would be cameras, public-relations employees, and private security in there with us, but it was just Amanda and me. I looked at her and said, "Where is everybody? You don't think it'll just be . . . ," and before I could finish my sentence, the five-time champion walked into the room. I knew I was about to receive an education on greatness that I couldn't learn from anyone else.

Kobe knew absolutely nothing about me except that I had planned a surprise wedding. Yet when he walked into the room, he sized me up like he was ready to play one-on-one in street clothes. We started off with small talk about his wife and kids. In the back of my head, I was getting a little nervous because I had rehearsed how I would tell him that I was training to be in the

NBA soon. As I was trying to take it all in, I kept thinking: *Abort mission. This is the worst idea you've ever had in your life. Are you really about to tell one of the greatest basketball players of all time that you're just going to randomly join the National Basketball Association? It's not a church league, Ryan. Do you really want to experience the most embarrassing moment of your life with Kobe? Be cool.*

I mustered up all the courage I could and finally just laid it out there . . .

"Hey, Kobe. So I'm working on this new documentary thing. It's called *Chasing Failure*. The idea behind it is that people are so afraid to fail that they do nothing at all . . ."

Kobe was staring at me with the most intense focus any man has ever given me, and I just couldn't get a solid read on what he was thinking.

"I'm out to show the world that failure ain't so bad after all. Instead of running from failure, what if people embraced it? I want to encourage every person I know to take their dreams off the shelf and stop being scared to lose."

At this point, I paused before continuing on, curious to see what Kobe's initial thoughts were . . . Nothing but crickets for ten seconds.

Kobe's silence felt like ten hours. But that's when I quickly discovered that Kobe had been listening intently to every word. After he had let what I said soak in, he responded with, "Absolutely. Every kid in America needs to hear that message. I wanna see that documentary."

Before I could respond, I had to take one last moment to consult with myself. *Crap, I told him that I was chasing failure, but I didn't tell him what I was actually going to do. He probably thinks I'm just gonna go run a 5K.*

After making his statement, he immediately went back into an intense listening mode. So I decided to let the cat out of the bag and said, "So the thing I'm going to be looking to fail at is . . . being in the NBA."

At this moment, I expected laughter or something along the lines of a sarcastic "Good luck, kid." Perhaps he would have even felt disrespected that I, a mere fan with lower-level collegiate basketball experience, would even think I belonged in the same league with him. Instead, what I got was four words that would push me even further down the journey of chasing failure. These four words would help me get over the fear. Kobe Bryant looked me in the face, without flinching or hesitating, and emphatically stated, "Yeah, man. Do it."

When your mom encourages you to chase your dream, it's nice, but it's what she's supposed to do. When your best friends urge you to shoot for the moon, it feels good to have their support, but it's not like you *have* to do it. But when a Hall of Famer tells you to go for it, you have now passed the point of no return.

"Chasing failure" went from a lofty notion to an irresistible destiny in just four words. As we wrapped up the last few moments of our hangout, he requested to see the film once it was completed. Kobe Bryant was waiting on me to start *Chasing Failure*. I bravely told him my plan, and then the only thing left was for me to figure out a way to actually accomplish it.

Did you know that Kobe, as of 2020, holds the record for the most missed shots in NBA history? In his book, *The Mamba Mentality*, Kobe said, "I wasn't scared of missing, looking bad, or being embarrassed. That's because I always kept the end result, the long game, in my mind. I always focused on the fact that I had to try something to get it, and once I got it, I'd have another tool in my arsenal. If the price was a lot of work and a few missed shots, I was OK with that."[1]

If isolated, that missed-shots statistic might make Kobe look like a failure, but in reality, that statistic, those failures, made him one of the best basketball players ever.

That's why I think you have to be willing to fall

short, miss a shot, or take a risk because chasing failure is more about *who* you're becoming than *what* you're achieving. Chasing success is circumstantial, whereas chasing failure is dependent not on circumstances but on your attitude, character, and mindset when the inevitable pitfalls, obstacles, and losses in life happen.

I'll never forget where I was on January 26, 2020, when I learned about Kobe Bryant's death. I was at lunch with two friends in Chicago when I saw a text message come through on my watch that said, "Is this fake news?"

I've never received more text messages and phone calls in one hour in my entire life than I did when TMZ broke the news that a Sikorsky S-76B helicopter crashed in Calabasas, California, around thirty miles northwest of downtown Los Angeles while en route from John Wayne Airport to Camarillo Airport for a youth basketball tournament. Nine people were on board, including Kobe, his thirteen-year-old daughter Gianna, the pilot, and seven other passengers. Everyone on the helicopter was killed on impact.

> YOU HAVE TO BE WILLING TO FALL SHORT, MISS A SHOT, OR TAKE A RISK BECAUSE CHASING FAILURE IS MORE ABOUT *WHO* YOU'RE BECOMING THAN *WHAT* YOU'RE ACHIEVING.

I still can't believe he's gone. I was looking forward to seeing his next chapter. He had recently won an Oscar and had so much more in the tank to make the world a better place. Looking back, I felt extremely privileged to have had an opportunity to hang out with the Black Mamba for ten minutes. I'm thankful for the impact he had on my life. He taught me the importance of criticism and how it can make you better, not bitter. He taught me that I don't have to choose between my career and my family by the way he constantly made time in his schedule for both. He taught me that sometimes you have to play hurt. He taught me that missing the mark is how you get better at hitting your target. And he taught me that you can't expect extraordinary results with ordinary habits.

The way Kobe approached his craft with grit and tenacity will forever be known as the Mamba Mentality. It's the mentality that would be required of me in my endeavors of chasing failure with the NBA.

KEY TAKEAWAY

You have to be willing to fall short, miss a shot, or take a risk because legacies aren't built without trying something that could fail.

THREE

REFRAMING FAILURE

Crisis doesn't create character; it reveals it.

—DENIS LEARY

In the NBA, there isn't a whole lot of "trying out," especially for twenty-eight-year-old guys off the street. If you want to be a successful and wealthy entrepreneur, you can go on *Shark Tank* and hope a multimillionaire or billionaire decides to invest in your business. If you're a fashion designer, you've got *Project Runway*. If you think you can dance or have an undiscovered talent in America, there are a couple of shows for that too. If you want to be a national recording artist, you can go on *The Voice* and pray that someone turns their chair around for you. But if you want to be in the NBA, you've got some hoops to jump through (pun intended). When you see an NBA player on television, chances are someone in that NBA organization has been watching him play since middle school.

I read a staggering stat from a 2014 *Boston Globe* article that said, "While the probability of, say, an American between 6–6 and 6–8 being an NBA player today stands at a mere .07 percent, it is a staggering 17 percent for someone 7 feet or taller."[1] I'm six foot three, which means my chances are even lower than .07 percent. With thirty teams in the NBA, and around fifteen roster spots on each team, that means there are roughly only 450 people playing in the NBA at one time. If you're in the NBA, you're in a very small club of athletes.

So let's imagine for a moment that I was eight years younger, twenty pounds more muscular, three inches taller, and in All-American shape, playing at a Division I school with a sharp sports agent representing me. My chances of actually making it to the NBA are still slim *at best*.

I'm very good at basketball, but "good at basketball" is relative to the context in which we're talking. How "good" am I according to NBA standards? The only way I could know for sure was to try. Initially, I didn't know *how* I was going to try out, but I knew I needed to be ready. I began training and dieting in case an opportunity arose, but I ended up with a strained IT band injury in my leg, and I could barely walk for three weeks.

This was rather disappointing. With no NBA workout in sight and now injured, I was failing . . . at chasing failure. So now a greater problem arose for me: I couldn't back down now, because I had already told my family, my friends, *and* Kobe Bryant that I was going to do this. I've learned when you tell people about your dream, it creates accountability for you to actually do something about it.

So while I was nursing my injury back to health but not knowing what step to take next, I did what most of us do whenever we don't know what to do: I Googled it. That's right. I searched the internet to find contact information for NBA teams' public-relations departments. I had no blueprint for how this would or could play out, but I knew I needed to start somewhere by reaching out to

WHEN YOU TELL PEOPLE ABOUT YOUR DREAM, IT CREATES ACCOUNTABILITY FOR YOU TO ACTUALLY DO SOMETHING ABOUT IT.

NBA teams. As I was beginning the process of emailing teams, I started having doubts, and negative thoughts flooded my mind:

Who do you think you are?
They're going to laugh at you.
They're going to think you're crazy.
Ryan, this is the NBA! What makes you think they're even going to respond?
You're wasting your time and theirs.
Ryan, this isn't how it works. NBA teams don't offer tryouts to complete strangers from email requests.

And I was right. NBA teams don't offer tryouts to complete strangers from email requests. But what did I really have to lose by sending the email? The reality for you and me is that the worst thing somebody can say to us at the door of opportunity is no. What's so scary about that word?

I don't know about you, but I've heard the word *potential* tossed around my whole life, and before I die, I'm just mildly curious to find out what mine is.

> **THE REALITY FOR YOU AND ME IS THAT THE WORST THING SOMEBODY CAN SAY TO US AT THE DOOR OF OPPORTUNITY IS NO.**

Maybe I was supposed to be in the NBA, or maybe I wasn't, but at age twenty-eight, it was something I had always wondered about but never actually tried. If you want to accomplish something you've never done, you will have to do things you've never done to get there. And at that point in my life, one thing I had never done was email NBA teams with a ludicrous inquiry. So I decided to give it a go.

I started with Boston, emailing my chasing-failure pitch to the public-relations executive of the Celtics. I told him this wouldn't just be a win for me, but it would be a win for their organization; because if they actually let me try out for their team, then that would mean they're in the business of believing in fans who are chasing their dreams. If we captured the experience, it would give that organization an opportunity to encourage each and every fan never to be afraid to fail.

I remember a friend asking me what I was doing that day. I told him, "I'm about to email the Boston Celtics and ask them to let me chase failure." He replied, "Are you serious?" Apparently, reaching out to the Boston Celtics out of the blue isn't normal, but I acted more confident than terrified—even though I most definitely felt more of the latter. Emailing an NBA team felt illegal to me. But all they could do was say no.

As I hit Send, I felt as though I was winning an MVP award.

I had taken a step in the direction of my dream. And I knew then that if I never got a tryout with an NBA team, at least I could say I was brave enough to get past my level of discomfort to send an email. Most people are too afraid to do just that.

Within thirty minutes of receiving the email, the Boston Celtics replied, informing me that they had discussed it internally but decided it wasn't for them. They wished me luck in the future with it all.

I was disappointed at first. I felt rejected. But my second thought was, *Wait a minute! Did the Boston Celtics just respond to my email?* I couldn't believe they even took the time to respond to my email, let alone actually read it. Their rejection gave me confidence to reach out to other NBA teams.

One team down. Twenty-nine to go.

I sent out three more emails, tweaking my pitch as I learned from the language used in the email I received from the Celtics. While I was waiting to hear back from the few NBA teams to whom I had reached out, my leg was getting back to full strength where I could at least start jogging again. In all reality, I began to believe my chasing-failure story would actually be about me *emailing all thirty NBA teams* and being told no each time.

The next team that responded was the Los Angeles Clippers. They let me know they thought it was a good idea, but in Hollywood's backyard, they get upwards of one hundred requests each month to do films and documentaries about their team, and at that time, chasing failure wasn't one of the themes they thought would be the best fit for their organization. Once again, I was still in shock that they would correspond with a complete stranger.

Two teams down. Twenty-eight to go.

My third email response came from the Phoenix Suns organization. As I braced for impact, I received an unexpected reply. The head of public relations said they were interested in the story and invited me to attend a workout with their head coach, Jeff Hornacek. They told me the best time for him would be ten days from the email. I was stoked because I had ten days to really prepare. Then they called and told me a better time for Coach Hornacek would actually be in three days, not ten. I was less stoked because I then only had seventy-two hours to prepare, but I still couldn't believe I was getting the opportunity of a lifetime. They also mentioned to me to bring my *camera crew*. Ha! I didn't have one. But I was sure I could find one—and his name was Chuck. I convinced him to take off work and go with me on a plane to Phoenix.

I was ecstatic that I was getting a chance to live out my dream. And I was excited to prove my inner critic wrong: *No, NBA teams don't usually offer tryouts to complete strangers from email requests . . . but sometimes they make an exception.* I had no idea what would happen in Phoenix, but before I was given the verdict of whether I was good enough or not to be in the NBA, I was confident in the person who was no longer afraid to lose. Chasing failure was taking me on a journey from dreaming to living.

CHASING FAILURE WAS TAKING ME ON A JOURNEY FROM DREAMING TO LIVING.

Three days later, on Monday morning, I showed up with my camera crew of one, Chuck, to the Talking Stick Resort Arena where the Phoenix Suns practice and play. As a huge basketball fan, I've been to my fair share of NBA games. I know what it feels like to smell the popcorn and hot dogs upon entering the many different stadiums and arenas to watch premier athletes do their thing. But it's an entirely different experience when you're walking into an arena to display what you can do with a basketball.

As security directed me down the hall toward the practice court, I passed pictures of Hall of Famers Charles Barkley and Michael Jordan from the 1993 NBA

Finals. I began to realize that I was walking down the same hall that some of the all-time greats had walked down many times. It was so nostalgic that I almost forgot why I was there.

The moment I walked onto that practice court, I knew I had about five minutes to transition from being a mere fan to a potential player.

Going from the 24 Hour Fitness gym on Sunday to an NBA practice court on Monday was a bit of a jump, and I was just trying to take it all in for what it was worth. Ready or not, it was time to see what I could do. Coach Jeff and I talked for a little bit, he sized me up like any coach would, and then he told me, "Get dressed." As I started lacing up my shoes to get ready to play, I slowly began to realize I might have been the shortest person in the entire gym besides Chuck. And I'm six foot three!

When I began the tryout, I was trying to shoot every shot perfectly instead of just going about how I would normally and comfortably shoot. I exerted unnecessary energy in an effort to not look tired. When I started playing with the guys in a three-on-three drill, I immediately felt that the speed, strength, size, and overall basketball IQ of every player there was astronomically greater than anything I'd ever experienced. As I said before, I'm very good at basketball, but this gym was a place for guys who are *outstanding*. They were elite. They were pros. I wasn't performing horribly, but there was nothing about my game that was *outstanding*.

When I scored once during one of the three-on-three drills, I felt like Michael Jeffrey Jordan. That was, until the guy I scored on blocked my next shot and scored on me three more times. With every missed shot, it became more apparent that I was indeed getting what I came for—*failure*. But it was great, and here's why: although these guys were better than I was that day, I wasn't afraid of them. Just because someone is better than you at something doesn't mean you have to live intimidated by them.

As the workout was coming to a close, Coach Jeff said to me, "You have a three-minute drill." The drill he was talking about was just pure sprinting up and down the court—for three minutes. He explained to me that getting down the ninety-four-foot court would count as one, and then coming back to the other end would be two. He then added more pressure by telling me how many lengths of the gym his best player can sprint in three minutes—thirty! His expectation for me during these three minutes was that I'd get around twenty-seven or twenty-eight! Oh, and then he did the math for me. He let me know that I basically had to cover all ninety-four feet in six seconds.

Thirty times.

For three minutes straight.

My main focus going into this drill was just to give it my all. That's why I was there. That's why I flew to Phoenix. I gave myself no other option than to deliver my very best. As I took off running as fast as I possibly could, something unexpected happened. Other players had been in the middle of their own drills all across the gym, but when I started my three-minute drill, the gym went silent. It was as if these players wanted to see this final drill. We were all curious to see if I could keep up with them, and this drill would be the true test. It made me just a bit more nervous knowing that not only was this being filmed, but now professional athletes were watching me, potentially, fail. One player shouted as I began the drill, "Whoa! You started too fast, brotha. You started waaaaay too fast!"

I was confused by this statement, because the task at hand was to cover the entire court in six seconds . . . thirty times. So how in the world could I have been going *too* fast?

I heard him, but I wasn't listening to him. I just knew I had to keep going. Within the first ninety seconds of the drill, my count was at thirteen, which had me on track to get around twenty-six. That number would put me in the middle of the Suns' big men and the average guard. But right at that ninety-second mark, my body hit a wall. I went from covering the entire court in six or seven seconds to covering it in twelve or thirteen seconds.

The best way I know to sum it up is to say that it was probably the most embarrassing moment of my life—and I had invited a cameraman to film it. And the full weight of failure truly began to set in with thoughts like these:

What in the world were you thinking coming here?
This is the NBA! What made you believe this would be a good idea?
Not only have you embarrassed yourself, but perhaps you've embarrassed Coach Jeff and the Phoenix Suns.
You don't belong in the same gym as any guy in here.

And then all of a sudden, as I was huffing and puffing up and down the court, I heard Coach Jeff on the baseline *cheering* for me. He started clapping for me and said, "Come on, Ryan! Finish strong. You got this. Finish strong. There's a trash can down here, and you can throw up later. Finish strong." And then the whole team started to put their hands together, cheering me on saying, "You got it, Ryan! Finish strong!"

As I finished the last thirty seconds of the drill,

running past the Phoenix Suns logo, I asked myself this question: *How did you get here?*

There are many places I could have been on this random September Monday afternoon, but I was running on the practice court of the Phoenix Suns. And I realized something that I'll never forget: *Chasing failure took me further than chasing success ever did.*

What was almost the most embarrassing moment in my life turned into one of the greatest moments I've ever had. I realized that, for three minutes, Coach Jeff wasn't just watching me run—he was coaching me as if I were one of his players. For three minutes, he was *my* coach. For three minutes, the Phoenix Suns was *my* team, and I've never been prouder to fail in my entire life. Something happened in Phoenix that I don't believe could have happened in the comfort of my own home: the fear of failure was broken off in my life.

CHASING FAILURE TOOK ME FURTHER THAN CHASING SUCCESS EVER DID.

Needless to say, I didn't make the team. But I did make a documentary. That opportunity and the story of *Chasing Failure* have led to greater opportunities than I could have ever imagined. Ironically, I now work with NBA teams off the court doing leadership development and executive coaching. Failure in Phoenix showed me a hard truth I didn't want to face at that time: there are a few things I'm better at than basketball. Sometimes we discover what we're supposed to do by process of elimination.

SOMETIMES WE DISCOVER WHAT WE'RE SUPPOSED TO DO BY PROCESS OF ELIMINATION.

Former Hewlett-Packard CEO and author Carly Fiorina was interviewed on *The ThriveTime Show* podcast about her book, *Find Your Way*. Her book outlines some of the lessons she learned from running for president of the United States. When asked about her presidential run on that podcast, she stated:

> I was prepared to win and I was prepared to lose . . . I also obviously knew that it was a really tall order. It was a very long shot. So while I put everything into it and believed I was highly qualified to do the job, I was also very prepared not to do the job and to go on and find other ways to make a difference consistent with what I believe.[2]

It wasn't president or bust for her. It was make a difference being president of the United States or make a difference not being president of the United States. What was most important for her is making a difference.

It's not Fortune 500 or bust for your business. It's adding value to your customers as a Fortune 500 company or adding value to your customers not as a Fortune 500 company. Adding value to your customers should be what is most important. It's not championship or bust for your team. It's your team doing the best they can and winning a championship or your team doing the best they can not winning a championship. But doing the best they can is what is important.

It's not Oscar or bust. It's not Grammy or bust. It's not getting verified on social media or bust. It's not a million subscribers or bust. Chasing failure is about giving your best to what you want to accomplish and being willing to live with the results. But if we're going to chase failure successfully (and yes, I know that sounds like a contradiction), we need to understand why we are chasing failure.

I'll never forget the day my *why* became crystal clear. It was the last day of my twenties, the day before my thirtieth birthday.

I was scheduled to speak to a group of financial planners about failure. A guy who had heard me speak at his church recommended me to his company's CEO because he thought I'd be a great fit at motivating their team. After the event, the guy pulled me aside and said, "Hey, I want you to know why I recommended that

CHASING FAILURE IS ABOUT GIVING YOUR BEST TO WHAT YOU WANT TO ACCOMPLISH AND BEING WILLING TO LIVE WITH THE RESULTS.

you speak to our team. I heard you tell your story at our church and I thought it was great, but it's bigger than that for me. It's personal. You see, my wife and I have a daughter who's dating a guy who we don't really approve of, but we try not to be too controlling of who she dates. He's on drugs and sleeps on the floor at his cousin's house. We don't have any common ground with him, but the one thing we do know is that he loves basketball. So after we heard you speak, we came home and showed him your *Chasing Failure* documentary."

At this point, he began to tear up.

He said, "He watched your video and called his father, who he had not spoken to in five years. They reconnected and began filling out job and junior college applications for the fall. He's now getting ready for college and has a job interview set up for next week. Oh, he also plans on trying to walk on to the basketball team. I want you to know you're not just a good speaker. You created something that pulled a young man's life off the floor."

And that was the moment my thirties got its theme,

and it's why I realized I wanted the next decade of my life to be about creating content that helps people get off the floor and moving in a direction that allows them to accomplish their dreams.

I wake up every single day believing somebody's life has hit rock bottom and they need to know there's hope.

It's why I keep speaking.

It's why I keep writing.

It's why I keep coaching.

It's why I keep recording.

I realize that every opportunity I get to present publicly what I've been working on privately is also an opportunity for failure. But my *why* sustains me when my doubts are noisy. If your *why* is compelling, you'll be willing to get it wrong a few times to get it right. When you're chasing failure, either you're learning or you're going to eventually win, and perhaps both.

KEY TAKEAWAY

The stronger your *why,* the more resilient you will become to setbacks and failures. Answer this question: Do you know your *why?*

FOUR

NEVER GIVE UP-*ISH*

If at first you don't succeed, destroy
all evidence that you tried.

—STEVEN WRIGHT

As a person who makes a living motivating people to move beyond their limitations, this is the part of the book where I'm supposed to tell you to *never give up*.

I'm then supposed to follow that up by telling you the Thomas Edison anecdote. You know that one, right? As an inventor, Edison made roughly a thousand unsuccessful attempts at inventing the light bulb. When a reporter asked, "How did it feel to fail a thousand times?" Edison replied, "I didn't fail a thousand times. The light bulb was an invention with a thousand steps."

It's a great story . . . *for Thomas*. I'm glad he didn't give up. While there are a lot of cases where I would tell you never to give up, there are some things you most definitely should not try a thousand times. Like trying out for *American Idol* and never making it to Hollywood once. If you didn't make it after the fifth time, there's a pretty good chance singing isn't your strong suit. "Never give up" is encouraging advice, but it's not always wise. I also believe it's just as important to know when you should *indeed* give up on one dream so you can grab hold of a better one. Chasing failure will help you discover what's not in the cards for you and prepare you for what actually is in the cards for you.

For a person to be a great classical pianist, they must possess certain characteristics: an excellent work ethic, diligence, and commitment to the craft. They must also have an in-depth knowledge of musical theory and the ability to read sheet music quickly. However, to be one of the greatest pianists in the world—one who is capable of selling out historic theaters like Carnegie Hall—a person must possess one more quality: they must be a prodigy. The best of the best possesses an unteachable ear for the music and a hand-eye coordination not found in the majority of the population. And at the Aspen Music Festival in 1971, a seventeen-year-old girl with dreams of becoming a professional pianist, capable of playing the world's greatest stages, realized she would never be good enough.

She had grown up playing piano her entire life, learning to read music before learning how to actually read. Beginning when she was only three years old, her grandmother taught her piano every day until she entered the University of Denver at age fifteen as a music major. She practiced diligently and daily, with dreams of playing Carnegie Hall. But upon attending the summer music school at the Aspen Music Festival and hearing her classmates play, she had a revelation. There was an intangible element these other prodigies had that she simply didn't possess. She watched twelve-year-olds play a piece of music by ear that had taken her a year to learn.

She returned to the University of Denver that fall looking for a new dream and a new major. It was then that she walked into a class on international relations with a focus on the Soviet Union. This class sparked a fire of interest in her that led to a highly success-ful career in academia, business, and, most notably, politics. Instead of growing up to become known as a world-famous pianist, she grew up to be addressed as "Condoleezza Rice, Secretary of State." Though she failed to accomplish her childhood dream of becoming a world-renowned pianist, Secretary Rice became the first African American woman named to the post of secretary of state; and by the time she left office, she held the record for most miles traveled in the office of secretary of state. On one special occasion, she even played piano for the queen of England. Rice said in an interview with *University of Denver Magazine* in 2010, "I've often said, sometimes your passion finds you instead of the other way around. I think this is a case where my passion found me."[1]

BEFORE YOU *NEVER GIVE UP* ON A DREAM, YOU SHOULD UNDERSTAND THE DISTINCTION BETWEEN WHAT IS SUPPOSED TO BE A CAREER AND WHAT IS SIMPLY A HOBBY.

Before you *never give up* on a dream, you should understand the distinction between what is supposed to be a career and what is simply a hobby. Is your dream supposed to be a side hustle or provide you a salary with health benefits?

I've seen a lot of people prematurely quit their day job for their side hustle when they could have kept their job *and* done something else during the weekends. I've seen people empty out their 401(k) for a hunch when they could have tested that hunch without losing their retirement. I've seen people take out a second mortgage on their home to start a business in a market they thought they understood. It's irresponsible to tell *everyone* to never give up, to throw caution to the wind, to relentlessly pursue their dreams without knowing whether or not that dream should be pursued.

It's popular to say, "Don't let anyone tell you what you can't do." I agree with that sentiment when a person is aware of their own strengths, weaknesses, and limitations. Yes, *then* you shouldn't allow someone else to put limitations on you. But are you self-aware enough to know if your goal is within your grasp?

- How do you know what should be a hobby and what should be a career?
- How do you know if you should quit your day job and go all in?
- What's a blueprint for knowing if you should pursue a dream or not?
- How can you figure out what you're *not* supposed to do?

I've quit positions before to pursue dreams, but I did so with a lot of calculations from an equation I call the Sweet Spot Matrix. Your sweet spot is where your passion, skillset, opportunity, and purpose intertwine.

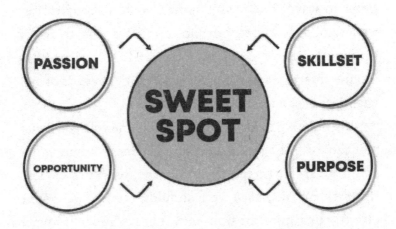

PASSION: WHAT DO YOU WANT TO DO?

For some, the answer to this question is clear. But I sit with a lot of people who have no clarity on this subject. Have you developed clarity around what you actually want to do?

In his book *Everything Is Spiritual*, Rob Bell wrote, "It's as if from an early age there is always someone pointing to a ladder and telling us to climb." He expounded on the various ladders we climb and then wrote, "Very few of us ever took a class that taught us how to know: Is this ladder even leaning up against the right building?"[2]

It would be a shame if you ended up doing a lot of climbing to land a dream job you have no passion for. I've found two things to be true: (1) God has a plan for your life, and (2) so do other people. Other people have a plan for what school you should go to, where you should work, and how you should live. How much time and energy will you give to what other people want you to do?

Andre Agassi shocked the sports world in 2009 when he released his autobiography, *Open*, and revealed that he hated tennis. How could one of the greatest tennis players of all time hate the game he was so good at? It was because tennis was a game forced upon Andre by his father. Tennis was his dad's plan, not Andre's plan.

It would be a tragedy if you woke up one day and realized you've been going along with someone else's plan you have zero passion for.

It's hard to fake passion. In relationships, when one partner is faking it or just going through the motions, the other can always feel the lack of passion. If you don't have passion, you won't fight for what you have once you get it. Passions can come and go, but you should

IT WOULD BE A TRAGEDY IF YOU WOKE UP ONE DAY AND REALIZED YOU'VE BEEN GOING ALONG WITH SOMEONE ELSE'S PLAN YOU HAVE ZERO PASSION FOR.

pay attention to what you're most consistently passionate about.

What's the thing you have natural energy for? What gets you in the zone? What's the thing that gets you out of bed in the morning with no coffee? What is the thing that causes you to lose track of time when you're doing it? What part of your current job do you love versus the part of your job you tolerate? The answers to these questions can serve as guiding lights to help you discover your passion.

We're taught at an early age to pursue what we feel is necessary in order to survive, to the extent that we often neglect what we actually want to do. But passion doesn't have to come at the expense of security. Could it be that there's a version of your life where you're able to be passionate about what you do *and* you're able to pay the bills?

Do you have clarity around what you're actually passionate about?

SKILLSET: WHAT ARE YOU GIFTED TO DO?

I actually have many passions. I have a passion to sing, play guitar, play basketball, cut hair, blog, write, do standup comedy, and create podcasts; but in no way am I gifted in all of the above.

Some people underestimate their abilities and skill-sets. They're better than they think they are. They're amazing vocalists who are too shy, modest, and humble to ever go on *American Idol*.

Some people, though, overestimate their abilities and skillsets. They're not nearly as good as they think they are. Mom has told them their whole life they're the best singer she's ever heard, and they may have ended up on *American Idol*—but as part of the blooper reel.

I speak a lot, and one interesting thing I've noticed when talking to audiences both large and small is that sometimes I'll burst into a song when telling a funny story. People rarely tell me afterward, "Man, you can really sing. You've got a great voice." Most of the compliments I've gotten in my career are around something I *said*, and almost never something I *sang*. No one has ever booed me, either, but I've heard some tones come out of my mouth that weren't exactly in a key suited for my voice.

I could get vocal lessons if I was really passionate about it. I could get guitar lessons if I really loved music. There may be something you've got a passion for that you need coaching in. Just because you're not naturally the best doesn't mean you shouldn't pursue it.

Before you make a decision about whether your dream is going to be a hobby or a career, you need an accurate assessment of your wiring, skillsets, and abilities. It's always going to go better for you if you enter into a conversation about your skillsets with humility rather than arrogance.

What are you good at? What do you want to be good at? You should give energy to improving either. If you're not sure how good you are, always err on the side of trying to get better. But for you to have a proper evaluation of your skillset, you need someone more credible than your mom to authenticate your giftedness. Only you can verify your own passion for something, but skillsets are typically verified by others. Do you know what you're good at? How do you know you're good at it?

Skillset can also be assessed with personality tests like StrengthsFinder or the Enneagram to help you better understand what you're naturally good at versus what you'll need nurtured.

ONLY YOU CAN VERIFY YOUR OWN PASSION FOR SOMETHING, BUT SKILLSETS ARE TYPICALLY VERIFIED BY OTHERS.

In light of where you want to go, are there technology skills you need to acquire? Are there people skills you need to learn? Are there leadership skills you need to start practicing?

You can have passion and a skillset, but without opportunity and purpose, it's not a sweet spot; it's just a spot.

OPPORTUNITY: WHAT DOORS
ARE ALREADY OPEN?

Are there any opportunities you have right now to do what you want to do that you also feel passionate and skilled to do?

I used to be frustrated not having the opportunities to do what I'm passionate about and felt skilled to do. Long before I was given opportunities to speak to thousands of people at one time, I was asked to speak to groups of ten or fewer. I gave the same energy to seven people that I would later give to seven thousand. Speaking at the small groups went well enough for me to be invited to speak to a few hundred people. One event speaking to a few hundred people led to an invitation to speak to fifteen thousand people.

Once when I was invited to a conference, I was given only seven minutes to speak. One seven-minute opportunity in that room turned into a forty-five-minute opportunity in another room to speak to forty thousand people. I want you to understand the power of valuing every opportunity to do the thing you love and feel gifted to do even when the opportunities don't look sexy. Don't forsake starting a podcast that only ten people listen to. You never know who one of those ten people might be or become. You never know who one of those ten people might be related to.

There's a lot of content out there about how to build your brand and come up with marketing strategies to get your name out there if you want to get more opportunities. But the greatest marketing strategy you can implement is simply doing a really good job at whatever you do. If you want more opportunities to do what you love, get really good at what you love. People ask me all the time how I get so many opportunities to speak. There's no secret sauce. I simply show up on time for my clients and do the best job I can. You'll be surprised at the number of opportunities that will come your way when you treat every opportunity like it's your last.

YOU'LL BE SURPRISED AT THE NUMBER OF OPPORTUNITIES THAT WILL COME YOUR WAY WHEN YOU TREAT EVERY OPPORTUNITY LIKE IT'S YOUR LAST.

Understand the difference between an opportunity that *already exists* and an opportunity you *should create*. A lot of dreamers often have to create opportunities.

The Broadway show *Hamilton* is a musical masterpiece that has grossed over $340 million worldwide. According to a 2015 *Vogue* article, the brilliant lyricist-composer-performer Lin-Manuel Miranda says he was "just chilling" in Mexico, reading a biography of Alexander Hamilton by Ron Chernow, when he had a sudden thought: "I was like, This is an album—no, this is a show. How has no one done this? It was the fact that Hamilton wrote his way off the island where he grew up. That's the hip-hop narrative. So I Googled 'Alexander Hamilton hip-hop musical' and totally expected to see that someone had already written it. But no. So I got to work."[3]

Miranda saw an opportunity to do something no one had ever done that aligned with his passion and skillset and jumped right on it. Perhaps there's something you've Googled that no one has done, but before you get to work, ask yourself: *Is this the right opportunity that aligns with my passion and skillset?*

When it comes to opportunity creation, you want to make sure you pay attention when other people say, "You should . . ."

"You should write a book."
"You should start a podcast."
"You should offer an e-course."
"You should speak to my agent."

I'm not saying act on all of them, but take heed of them. I got into executive coaching because executives would hear my messages and say, "Our company needs to hear that, and I need help implementing your message into my life." So I started crafting proposals and workshops I thought could add value to people. In this instance, passion came after an opportunity while the skillset was TBD. But I went for it anyway because there was only one way to find out if I was good at it. I didn't show up to these companies good at what I do. I showed up not afraid to try.

What do people (besides your parents) encourage you to do?

I have a friend who called to tell me he wanted to start an online course for leaders. I knew he had the ability to do it, but my question for him was, "Who's asking you for leadership advice?" I didn't ask the question to offend him but to save him money in the event his answer was *nobody*. Online courses aren't cheap to create. *E-books are.* Go crush it *or blow it* with an e-book when the stakes are rather low. If you see the responses to the e-book are good, then take it up another level, but proven success is a good indicator for you to know if you should pursue higher heights.

Should you start flipping houses because you were inspired watching HGTV? I think you should first investigate what real-estate opportunities currently exist in your region.

Should you move to Hollywood and live out your dream of becoming an actor or actress? I think you should first audition for some local gigs to test the waters before you move to one of the most expensive places to live in the country. You could also start a YouTube channel where you don't need to win an audition. All you have to do is hit Record. It's free, and you can still keep your job.

You want to be able to understand the risk involved before you move forward with anything. I know I'm supposed to try to get you to take a leap of faith, but sometimes it's better to take a leap of wisdom.

What opportunities do you need to create, and what opportunities do you need to steward better?

PURPOSE: WHAT WERE YOU BORN TO DO?

This may be the most important component in finding your sweet spot. If what you do doesn't have purpose, no matter what you do, you'll always live unfulfilled. It's possible to engage in work you love, get paid for what you're skilled at doing, and capitalize on opportunities to showcase your work; but if it's not *meaningful work*, you may find yourself applauded and miserable at the same time. You were born to do something

YOU WERE BORN TO DO SOMETHING MEANINGFUL.

meaningful. We were all actually born with a deep need to do something of great significance.

Maslow's hierarchy of needs, developed in the 1940s, helps us understand our needs as humans. This motivational theory in psychology comprises a five-tier model, depicted in a pyramid shape. Changes were later made in the 1960s and 1970s from a five-stage model to a seven-stage model and then to one with eight stages.

MASLOW'S HIERARCHY OF NEEDS

Transcendence

Self-actualization

Aesthetic needs

Cognitive needs

Esteem needs

Belongingness and love needs

Safety needs

Biological and physiological needs

Starting from the bottom, we first learn we have *biological and physiological needs*—air, food, drink, shelter, warmth, sex, sleep, and so forth.

Second, we all have *safety needs*—protection from elements, security, order, law, stability, freedom from fear.

Third, we all have a need for *love and belonging*—friendship, intimacy, trust, acceptance, receiving and giving affection and love.

Fourth, we all have *esteem needs*—which Maslow classified into two categories where we have a need for esteem for oneself and for reputation or respect from others.

Then we have *cognitive needs*—knowledge and understanding, curiosity, exploration, need for meaning and predictability.

Then we move into all of us having *aesthetic needs*—appreciation and search for beauty and balance.

Some of our highest needs are where I believe we can find our purpose.

Maslow then suggested that you and I have *self-actualization needs*—realizing personal potential, self-fulfillment, seeking personal growth and peak experiences.

And the highest needs we have are actually *transcendence needs*—the need to help others reach their potential.

Our purpose in life is to reach our full potential and help others reach theirs as well.

The final question I have for you in discovering your sweet spot is, "Does what you want to accomplish help others reach their potential?"

After losing his first wife to cancer, Daron Babcock fell into depression and started picking bar fights and snorting lines of coke. Though he was a successful businessman with a six-figure salary, he felt unfulfilled and aimless.

Daron decided to go with his friend one Saturday to volunteer with a group in South Dallas called H.I.S. BridgeBuilders that mentored men coming out of the prison systems. He had no idea what he was getting into but enjoyed that first Saturday so much he kept going back every week. What started off as just volunteering two hours on Saturdays eventually became a calling that led this successful businessman and father of two to quit his job, sell his 3,600-square-foot home in Frisco, Texas, and move into a Habitat for Humanity house in Bonton (an area in South Dallas) with a two-time convicted felon.

Daron found that Bonton had two major issues he could do something about: unemployment and poor health. Men who were in and out of prison found it difficult to get a job. And Bonton's cardiovascular disease rate was 54 percent higher than that of the City of Dallas. Diabetes was 45 percent higher. The chance of having a stroke was 61 percent higher. Cancer was 58 percent higher. Bonton was considered a *food desert*, an urban area in which it is difficult to buy affordable or good-quality fresh food. In contrast, an area with supermarkets or produce shops is a food oasis.

When Daron moved into the neighborhood, 63 percent of Bonton residents lacked personal transportation—and the nearest grocery store was a three-hour round-trip bus ride away. So the most accessible option for them was one of three beer and wine stores that sold overpriced, outdated, processed foods. When that's your diet, the impact on your health is devastating.

Daron started small by planting a garden next to his house, with no greater vision than it would give the guys something to do every day and food to take home at night. Daron began selling or bartering the food to people in the community so they could eat better, get healthier, and eventually land stable jobs.

Habitat for Humanity took notice of the impact Daron was making, so they donated two lots in the area to expand the garden. The City of Dallas then ended up donating six more lots behind those to make the garden even bigger. Daron's passion, skillset, opportunity, and purpose aligned to help him make a move from the suburbs of Dallas to a food desert to make a difference in other people's lives.

If writing a book, being a professional athlete, creating a course, running for office, getting a law degree, opening a bakery, starting a nonprofit, or whatever it is you want to do helps others accomplish their potential . . . then do it.

My friend, I wake up every day with a fire in my soul to make a difference. I'm not just a motivational speaker. I'm a *motivated* speaker. I'm motivated to help people find their purpose, and I don't believe they can do that without connecting with their Creator. I have a passion for it. I have a skillset to pull it off. I'm given opportunities I don't deserve to do it. And I know I was born to do it. I'm living in my sweet spot.

I'd love to tell you to never give up. But I'd rather tell you to fail at all the things early so you can chase your purpose and find your sweet spot.

So, what's your dream? What's your sweet spot? How do the two fit together? Once you realize your dream and know that it aligns with your passion, skills, opportunities, and purpose, you can begin to take active steps toward chasing failure.

In order to chase our dreams practically and realistically, keeping our sweet spot in mind, we need to count the cost of following our dreams.

KEY TAKEAWAY

Your sweet spot is where your passions, skillset, opportunity, and purpose intertwine. Chasing failure will help you discover what's *not* in the cards for you and prepare you for what *is* in the cards for you.

WHO *WANTS* TO BE
A MILLIONAIRE?

> Become a millionaire not for the million dollars,
> but for what it will make of you to achieve it.
>
> —JIM ROHN

We love the word *million*.

It's primarily used to describe an amount of money one would need to have in their bank account to join an elite class of people.

I have this friend who makes about $950,000 a year. He's loaded for sure. But he doesn't make a million a year. *I almost make a million dollars a year* doesn't have the same ring to it.

The word *million* has the same effect on the internet. Most social media users would love to have a million followers. Online businesses would love to have a million customers. YouTubers would love to have a million subscribers with a million views on each upload. Singer-songwriters would love to have a million downloads.

I remember when our "Surprise Wedding" video hit over a million views on YouTube and I started getting text messages from friends saying: "You made it."

Frequent fliers would love to have a million miles accumulated with their go-to airline. If you have any loyalty rewards program with any department store or hotel brand, wouldn't you love to have a million points with them?

Million is the gold standard for just about everything. Whenever I talk with dreamers, the word *million* usually comes up in some form or another. It especially comes up with authors. When you're first putting pen to pad, it's hard not to envision your name on the *New York Times* Best Sellers list. Most authors practice their *Oprah* interview before they even finish the book.

But there's an extreme amount of naivety and optimism around selling a million books.

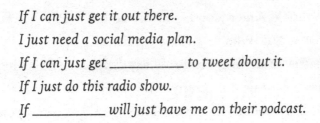

If I can just get it out there.
I just need a social media plan.
If I can just get _____ to tweet about it.
If I just do this radio show.
If _____ will just have me on their podcast.

Those initiatives are plausible, but they most likely won't help an author sell a million copies of their book. They'd need a lot of things to go right to sell that many books. Saying your goal is to sell a million copies of a book is like saying your goal is to win the lottery. Unfortunately, it's just not a realistic goal.

According to Bowker, the combined total of self-published print books and e-books with registered ISBNs grew from almost 1.2 million in 2017 to more than 1.6 million in 2018.[1] That's not even including books from major publishers. According to *Publishers Weekly*, out of all the bestselling print books published in 2019, only three of them sold more than a million copies in that year. So when we do the math, an author's chances of selling a million copies of a book are dismal at best.

Authors desiring to sell a million copies of a book tend to fall for at least one of two traps, and usually both. First, they believe that selling a million copies of a book is a more important goal than actually writing a great book. And second, they avoid counting the cost of what it will take to pull off that feat.

In the dreaming phase, everything is free. When people dream of doing anything *million*, they usually dream only about the perks. They rarely dream about the pressure, the criticism, the impact money has on all relationships, and, in some cases, the lawsuits. In Will Smith's YouTube video titled "The Truth About Being Famous," he said, "I get sued probably fifteen times a year. I have lawyers on a monthly retainer just because you get sued so much when you're famous."[2]

IN THE DREAMING PHASE, EVERYTHING IS FREE.

And people definitely don't dream about the taxes of doing anything *million*. Because the tax rate for anybody making over $518,400 as of 2020 is upwards of 37 percent.

Make a million and get a check ready for $370,000 to Uncle Sam. Not to mention your state taxes, unless you're a fellow Texan like me or you live in one of the other handful of states where you're not required to pay state income taxes. But if you happen to live in California, like Stephen Curry, your state tax is around 12 percent.[3]

In 2017, ESPN partnered with a sports tax expert from PKF O'Connor Davies to analyze the salaries of the NBA's highest-paid players. They reported from Stephen Curry's gross pay of $34,682,550, he'd have to pay $11,655,683 in federal taxes and another $4,105,453 in state taxes.[4]

You might think, *Well, he still has about $20 million left over.* Did I mention his agent? Or his publicists? What it takes to be Stephen Curry means more than just how well he handles a basketball. The late Notorious B.I.G. said it best: *Mo' money. Mo' problems.*

Are you sure you *want* to be a millionaire? Are you sure you want hundreds of thousands of people praising you one week and criticizing you the next? Are you sure you want people to dedicate whole blogs to criticizing your work? Are you sure you want to win? Are you sure you want to accomplish your goal? Because once you do, you might have to become a different person.

It's important to understand that every single one of our goals, hopes, and dreams has a price tag on it. Do you know what yours is? If we're honest, what do most of us want? We want a successful person's glory without their pain. We want their accolades and highlights without their grind and waiting in line.

> **WE WANT A SUCCESSFUL PERSON'S GLORY WITHOUT THEIR PAIN.**

A mentor taught me once that whenever I encounter someone I believe to be successful, always ask them the question, "What does it cost to be you?"

How much time away from their family does it cost to be them? How many hours of practice does it cost to be them? How much sleep did they give up to be who they are?

Who do you know who is successfully doing now what you want to do later? You will want to study where they've failed and what they learned. You then will want to see what they're doing that you're not. This is how you will find out what it takes to pull off your dream.

I want to equip you with five questions that will help you count the cost of your dream. These questions will help you understand what it takes to get from where you are to where you want to be.

I. HOW MUCH *TIME* IS REQUIRED?

You cannot overestimate the time required to achieve a dream. In his book *Outliers*, Malcolm Gladwell outlines what he calls the 10,000-Hour Rule, which he considers the key to success in any field, as simply a matter of practicing a specific task that can be accomplished with twenty hours of work a week for ten years. He found that the individuals who mastered a craft in their field had put in at least ten thousand hours of work before they were deemed experts.[5]

One of the common denominators of successful people is they don't get a lot of sleep. When Kobe Bryant was in his prime, younger players would ask to work out with him. If by chance he would give them the opportunity to do so, he'd tell them to meet him at his house at 4:00 a.m. *Be careful what you ask for.*

Steve Harvey wears many hats as a producer, comedian, game show host, talk show host, and radio host. Many people in the entertainment industry aspire to accomplish what Steve has, but only few have what it takes to handle his schedule, which routinely starts at 4:00 a.m. and ends around 11:00 p.m.

Talent can only get you so far, but hard work will keep you steady when you arrive at your destination.

You don't need to be an expert on day one, but you can put in expert time on day one. You can't control that you're not where you want to be yet, but you can control putting in the time it takes to get there.

> **TALENT CAN ONLY GET YOU SO FAR, BUT HARD WORK WILL KEEP YOU STEADY WHEN YOU ARRIVE AT YOUR DESTINATION.**

It's important to know how much time the pursuit of a project will cost you in terms of time away from the people who matter most. I'm not sure what your goal is, but my guess would be that to achieve it, you're going to actually have to give up something in your schedule to pull it off. I originally scheduled my time to write this book strategically after the 2020 NBA playoffs would normally have been played. Of course, thanks to a pandemic, I am now writing this book *during* the NBA playoffs, which meant I had to make a decision about where my time would go. Even during years when I am not writing a book, there are seasons when I cut out hobbies altogether to accomplish a goal.

This is where I would actually suggest you create a *To-Don't-Do* list. That's right. I want you to write down a couple of items and/or activities on a piece of paper or on your device that you are not going to do this week so you can make time for what you want to accomplish.

I've had to walk away from some endeavors because of the time commitment. The reward of the endeavor succeeding at the highest level wasn't worth the time away from my family with an already full schedule.

It's vitally important to know how much time is required to win. And if you don't know and you're guessing, always err on the side of it being more than what you've anticipated.

Time management is perhaps the most underrated component of winning. I believe your calendar and schedule have the greatest impact on your success or lack thereof.

We live in a world where everyone feels like they have a busy schedule. Talking about how busy we are is almost a part of our everyday vernacular. In fact, the busier we sound, the more celebrated we are. Most people are owned by their schedules rather than them owning their schedules. They allow things to just happen.

We should treat our time like we treat our money. Budget it. When you don't have a plan for your money, it ends up getting spent on things that don't set you up for success financially in the future. If we don't make a plan for our time, someone or something will eat it up just like our finances. Set up your schedule for success. You do this by being intentional and not letting entertainment eat up your time. As "busy" as we say we are, it's amazing what we actually find and make time to do.

We make time for HGTV.

We make time for social media.

We make time for Netflix and the ever-growing list of new streaming services.

WE SHOULD TREAT OUR TIME LIKE WE TREAT OUR MONEY. BUDGET IT.

We make time for sports.

You and I make time for the things we want to do the most.

I know people who make excuses for why they can't accomplish their goals but can finish eight seasons of *Game of Thrones* in two weeks. Did you know that all eight seasons run a total of 4,201 minutes? That's seventy hours! Did you know that all nine seasons of *The Office* run 4,376 minutes? That's 72.9 hours. And I know people who have watched both shows all the way through twice. Yet . . . we "don't have time" to figure out email marketing and do what we need to do to move forward.

The question you have to ask yourself is this: Am I making time for my goals?

Sports and entertainment aren't bad. I love both. But I'm incredibly intentional with my schedule because my calendar is in alignment with my goals.

2. WHAT *DISCIPLINES* ARE REQUIRED?

Most people fail due to a lack of discipline. The funny thing about personal disciplines is they often bleed into professional disciplines. For example, working out may have nothing to do with producing an album on the surface, but it does indirectly affect the success of the project because it has a direct impact on your physical health.

Researchers at the Mayo Clinic have cited that exercise improves mood, boosts energy, and promotes better sleep. One article the clinic published said, "Physical activity stimulates various brain chemicals that may leave you feeling happier, more relaxed and less anxious. You may also feel better about your appearance and yourself when you exercise regularly, which can boost your confidence and improve your self-esteem."[6]

What discipline is required for you to succeed?

Is it waking up earlier?
Is it staying up later?
Is it eating healthier?
Is it saving more money?
Is it making more time in your schedule?

One discipline I've acquired over the past few years is either listening to or reading one book a week. Of course, I've failed this many weeks, but there have also been weeks when I read more than one book. The point is, I've created an essential discipline to keep me fresh for accomplishing my goals. You're not going to be awesome at anything by accident. So what intentional discipline do you need to implement that aligns with your goals?

3. WHAT *FINANCIAL INVESTMENT* IS REQUIRED?

I've had several friends who have incredible app ideas with zero resources to pull them off. They have a great idea, but they don't speak venture capitalist. They can have a winning concept, but that doesn't mean they speak marketing. Understanding the financial implications of your idea is crucial for its long-term success.

Depending on what the idea is, you just have to do the math. You can also Google the math on what the average cost of building an app is. I just did and here's what I found: a single app development and deployment may cost anywhere between $50,000 and $1,000,000, and it can take from half a year to upwards of a year to be completed.

That's quite a range, but at least you know what the ground floor is for your app.

There have been reports that LeBron James spends $1.2 million or more a year to take care of his body.

Most people say he has God-given talent. That may be true, but he also has $1.2 million that he is investing into his body to be the best he can be. Many young basketball players want to be in the NBA, but often they aren't willing to eat healthy and take care of their bodies enough to be elite.

To run for president of the United States of America as an independent candidate, you'd need to gather about five thousand signatures, then petition each state to get your name on the ballot and raise at least $10 million to be a respectable contender. And that would just be the beginning.

Whenever you start making money, you'll be tempted to spend money rather than reinvest into your idea to make it better and scale it so more people can experience it. There are bestselling authors who have invested heavily in their marketing plans, sometimes pouring their whole book advance into a marketing strategy. Because sometimes that's what it takes to make an idea successful, but you have to be willing to let go of temporary income for a long-term payoff.

When starting a small business, you don't have to think about all these things right away, but you at least want to see these costs on the horizon in the event your small business grows big:

Incorporation fees
Permits and licenses
Website and logo
  design
Brochure and business
  card printing
Signage
Rent
Payroll
Taxes
Training and
  leadership
  development
Legal services
Loan payments
Insurance payments
Utilities
Marketing costs

A CEO friend of mine gave me some great advice when I was a young entrepreneur. He said, "Ryan, there are two people you can't overpay. Your lawyer and your accountant. Those are the two people that keep you out of jail." Duly noted, my friend.

4. WHAT DO I NEED TO *LEARN*?

One of the biggest mistakes someone can make in trying to accomplish any goal is attempting to do so without researching how others have had similar success. This is a class we have to show up for and learn from others' failures.

You have more access to education and information on your smartphone than previous generations had in a library.

There's a podcast for every industry.

You can literally YouTube how to build a house.

I've seen online courses on "What to Text a Girl You Like," "How to Biohack Your Brain's Health," and "Learning the Art of Clowning."

There's something on the internet for everyone.

YOU HAVE MORE ACCESS TO EDUCATION AND INFORMATION ON YOUR SMARTPHONE THAN PREVIOUS GENERATIONS HAD IN A LIBRARY.

But while Google may be a great place to start, it's a horrible place to end.

The reason people often fail is because they neglect doing the homework necessary for them to know the blueprint that will help them win. Many people don't have the luxury of having a mentor to show them the ropes or model for them what it takes to accomplish their goals, but we have the ability to get all the information we need to be successful if we're willing to do our homework.

There are two types of learning: formal and informal. Some achievements require formal education. Some roles require letters before and after a person's name. And if you're performing a triple bypass surgery, you should have as many letters associated with your name as possible.

But a large portion of the dreamers I hear from have hopes in their heart that require more informal education. The information they need is found in books, online courses, or a conference.

My brother Corey didn't get a college degree, but he did get a Certificate of Diversity and Inclusion from Cornell University. And now he helps many organizations create cultures of diversity and inclusion at a high level. It cost him some money, but not the same amount of debt he would have incurred getting a four-year degree from Cornell. The important component for my brother is that he did what he *needed to do* to be equipped for the *meaningful work he wanted to do.*

I've heard so many sentiments around what people don't know or don't understand.

I don't understand social media ads.
I don't get real estate.
I don't know how to do email campaigns.
What's a sales funnel?
Should I get on TikTok?
My friend told me I need a Twitter account.

Your idea may not require you to be social media or technologically savvy. But your idea may require you to learn leadership. Someone in the world is writing a book, blog, or course to help you learn what you need in order to win. It's your job to find it. You have to know what your future requires you to learn. If you want to go somewhere new, you are going to have to learn something new.

5. *WHO* DO I NEED TO KNOW?

The old saying goes, "It's *who* you know, not *what* you know." The most underrated cost of pulling off what you want to accomplish in the future is the relationships you build along the way. I'm not suggesting brownnosing. I'm not saying you need to learn to play golf. I'm saying you want to do your best to treat everyone you encounter with dignity, respect, and honor, because the way people make decisions about who they want to work with and who they want to give contracts to is often based on relationships more than quality of products.

Ninety-five percent of the biggest opportunities I've ever had came as a result of a relationship I've had for years that I never expected anything from. I'm not being someone's friend today so I can cash in a favor later. I aim to be a good person and add value to everyone around me, and people take notice of those in their lives who have treated them well.

I'll never forget when, at age thirty-two, I found myself speaking at one of the largest mortgage companies in the country. When I began to trace back how in the world I had even gotten in the room, I realized I arrived there as a result of a relationship I started building when I was a sophomore in high school.

My teacher's name was Chad Bruegman. He was my Bible teacher. He encouraged me and believed in me. He eventually became one of the leaders of a church in Denver, Colorado, called Red Rocks Church. We remained friends throughout the years, and one day he recommended that one of their departments have me come speak for an event. When I arrived in Denver, he then asked me to speak at their weekend services, offering me the slot he was supposed to fill that weekend. *That's no small opportunity.*

In the audience of thousands that weekend was the president of a mortgage company who later invited me to speak at her company. Had it not been for Chad, I would have never gotten to speak at that mortgage company. Yes, I know I work my butt off, but so do a lot of people. Much more than anything else, my career is primarily a product of the relationships I've built throughout the years.

Sometimes going to a conference or to a networking event is required. But there's no substitute for being a good person and treating every person you meet like they've got a million bucks in their pocket.

Author and leadership guru John Maxwell often talks about putting a 10 on other people's heads. What he means by that is he gives each person a score of 10 (on a scale of 1 to 10) when he meets them. From the very beginning, he assumes the best about them and chooses to believe that about them. This is how you develop the kind of influence over time to set you up to win.

Have you counted the cost? And are you willing to pay it?

There's good news and bad news. The bad news is you could still fail after all of that. The good news is you'll have learned more than a college degree could ever give you.

An alumnus from my alma mater, Ben Peters, spent months on data analytics, research, and forecasting to decide whether or not he should step into the Airbnb business model. When his findings told him it was worth the risk, he purchased a small home in Minneapolis and began renting it out.

Though his rental was booked solid, it ended up failing miserably due to unexpected events. Though he had done all the right research and counted the cost, he hadn't seen a 2020 pandemic coming. Once stay-in-place and quarantine orders were lifted, he was able to get it booked solid again, but then George Floyd was killed and Minneapolis riots destroyed what was left of his Airbnb business.

He then wrote this online: "But that's why I'm going to succeed. You either win, or you learn. And I definitely didn't win on this investment! But where there is no risk, there is no reward. I risked it, it didn't work out, and I learned a ton! And now I know what to look for, and where to look for it (on my next Airbnb investment)."

Are you willing to pay for something now that could fail but will give you what you need to succeed later?

ARE YOU WILLING TO PAY FOR SOMETHING NOW THAT COULD FAIL BUT WILL GIVE YOU WHAT YOU NEED TO SUCCEED LATER?

Dreams are costly, but they are the best investment. Even if you fail in one area or another, you know that you put your resources toward something worthy.

Have you counted the cost? And are you willing to pay it?

Achieving your dream is going to require sacrifice and effort. You will need to consider the time, discipline, money, knowledge, and network you need before going after your dreams. Once you know what it will take, you are ready to start taking steps to have your dream become a reality. A dream without a plan is just a hope. I want to help you figure out a game plan so that every day you can get one step closer to chasing failure, achieving your dreams, and living the most fulfilling life possible.

KEY TAKEAWAY

It's important to understand that every single one of our goals, hopes, and dreams has a price tag on it. Answer this question: Who do you know who is successfully doing now what you want to do later? You will want to study where they've failed and what they learned. You then will want to see what they're doing that you're not.

SHAME *OFF* YOU

Success isn't permanent, and failure isn't fatal.

—MIKE DITKA

I have a confession.

This is actually the *fifth edition* of this book. I'm not talking about the fifth *draft*. There are hundreds of those. What I mean is, this is the fifth time I've published a book with this title. I'm not supposed to tell you that. I'm supposed to pretend like I'm a bestselling author and it's always been that way. But that's not the truth.

Yeah, I've failed . . . *writing a book on failure* . . . four times.

The first time I wrote *Chasing Failure*, it was fewer than sixty pages, and it was basically my journey of getting a workout with the Phoenix Suns sprinkled with a few inspirational quotes. I had a friend design the cover for it, I self-published it, and I thought it was brilliant. However, when the books arrived, I was disappointed in how the cover came out due to the unattractive glossy finish of the book that felt flimsy to me. The pages themselves felt cheap. Nevertheless, I gave copies to a few people at my church and, in general, received a positive response. But there was one honest person who pulled me to the side and told me what every author fears: "I found three typos."

I was so embarrassed. Now I had a book with a mediocre cover and three typos, and I had purchased a thousand of them. *Can you sell a book that has typos? Maybe.*

Every writer has a draft of something they've published where they substituted "there" for a "their," or "it's" for an "its." If you've ever published anything on the internet, you probably have experienced those people out there who feel like their life's calling is to police the grammar of the world around them.

The reality every author has to face is the fact that typos happen. Typos happen even after several rounds of editing. And this doesn't just happen to rookies. In the first edition of the first Harry Potter book, the list of school supplies for Hogwarts includes "1 wand" twice. *Wizards don't need two wands.*

In one of Shakespeare's less-famous plays, *Cymbeline*, there's a female character whose first name is Imogen. Her character was developed based on someone from British history. The only issue with her name is that it wasn't Imogen. It was Innogen with two *n*'s. Apparently the two *n*'s were mistaken for an *m* and the name ended up being printed as "Imogen" for all time.

I guess you can sell books with typos.

Nevertheless, I fixed the typos and reprinted a second edition and allowed the disappointing glossy cover to remain. Six months later I was invited to speak at the third-largest church in America. You'd think that'd be exciting, but the larger the opportunity you're given, the more scrutiny you invite to your work. While there, a lady who asked me to sign her copy of the latest edition of my book also told me what every second-edition author fears: "I found four typos in your book."

These were four new typos that neither I, a few editors, nor a few other grammatically astute individuals found in the first or second editions. So I printed a third edition and upgraded the pages to feel a little bit more legit.

Then I read a review of the book online. (This is a

> **THE LARGER THE OPPORTUNITY YOU'RE GIVEN, THE MORE SCRUTINY YOU INVITE TO YOUR WORK.**

bad habit.) One buyer said he was disappointed in the length of the book and didn't even consider it a real book. That sentiment sent me searching for a fourth edition where I added three chapters that offered some spiritual applications. I took this fourth edition as an opportunity to finally update the cover and make the book look and feel how I really wanted. I printed a few hundred of that fourth edition, but honestly, I was actually embarrassed that I even had to have a fourth edition. I felt shame and never actually marketed it. I wasn't chasing failure with my fourth edition; I was falling into it.

My message is sometimes easy to give but hard to live. I wanted to inspire people with my words, but shame kept me from promoting the fourth edition of my book—shame and a couple of misplaced commas.

When it comes to pursuing something outside of our comfort zone, the largest emotional hurdle any of us faces is *shame*. Shame and failure often go hand in hand.

The technical term for the fear of failure is *atychiphobia*. The American Psychological Association defines *atychiphobia* as the persistent and irrational anxiety about failing to measure up to the standards and goals set by oneself or others. This may include anxiety over academic standing, losing a job, sexual inadequacy, or loss of face and self-esteem.

Here's a situation you may have found yourself in: An opportunity comes up in life, whether work or personal. You know someone similarly situated to you who would face and perhaps even enjoy the challenge. For you, though, it feels like a threat. Your biology even responds this way, releasing adrenaline and cortisol into your bloodstream.

Why is this? Studies show that individuals with a high degree of fear of failure view these events as judgment-oriented experiences. For you, it's not just your reputation or job on the line but your entire identity. And when your identity is at risk, you enter survival mode. Fear looks at the future through the lens of failure, and the end result is an emotional, mental, and spiritual black hole with a one-word name: *shame*. Though fear is often the first offender, shame is the real killer. Shame's banner campaign is not "you failed" but "*you* are a failure." Failure is an event, not an outfit. Just because you went there doesn't mean you have to wear it.

Instead of serving as a stepping-stone to success

(its primary redeemable quality), failure becomes an unacceptable outcome when paired with shame. To preserve every shred of self-worth and dignity possible, you strictly hedge against any opportunity to experience a future failure.

> **FAILURE IS AN EVENT, NOT AN OUTFIT. JUST BECAUSE YOU WENT THERE DOESN'T MEAN YOU HAVE TO WEAR IT.**

The real twist comes when your avoidance of failure feels like a failure itself. This is when the spiral really . . . well . . . spins. You're stuck between a rock and an even bigger rock. If you try and fail, shame will catch you, which your brain tells you is an inevitable outcome. If you don't try, the lack of effort is in itself failure, and shame is there to greet you all the same.

We need to chase failure, and we can't stay in our comfort zone to do so. And the answer isn't just to ignore shame. We need to recognize our shame triggers so we can respond to them appropriately and make sure our passion isn't extinguished in the process.

Shame isn't random. There are specific events, moments, and even people that can be shame triggers for us. We all have different ones. For some of us shame is triggered when we see other people getting complimented. I call this *phantom discouragement.*

It's when someone compliments your friend's work, so you believe yours is trash. Nobody said your work was garbage, but because you didn't hear that your contribution added value, you then believe it has none.

Most of our triggers in this arena are generally in the area of how people respond to us. Someone not texting you back might be a trigger for you. Getting on social media might be a trigger for you.

Storyteller and researcher Dr. Brené Brown has done extensive research on *shame triggers*. The data she's collected suggest that a woman's primary shame trigger is often physical appearance, and for men it is the fear of being perceived as weak.[1] If we can identify our insecurities and control them before they control us, we position ourselves for shame not to have a hold on our destiny. The only thing to do is stay in your "comfort zone," which is simply a nice substitute phrase for "prison." I want to help you get out and get shame off you so you can start being who you were meant to be. There are three things you can do to fight against shame.

I. DON'T EXPECT PERFECTION

When we expect ourselves to be perfect, which is impossible, it sets us up to experience more shame when we fail or do something wrong. With social media broadcasting our lives around the world, many of us feel paralyzed to act because we are afraid of not being perfect.

In the Netflix documentary *The Social Dilemma*, social psychologist, professor, and author Jonathan Haidt talked about the adverse effects of social media on Generation Z: "A whole generation is more anxious, more fragile, more depressed. They're much less comfortable taking risks. The rate at which they get driver's licenses have been dropping. The number who have ever gone out on a date or had any kind of romantic interaction is dropping rapidly."[2]

The purpose of social media was to help us connect—to be more *social* with one another. But the more we use it, the further we get away from its original design. Most people get online to connect, but they leave not only feeling disconnected but also with an extreme case of envy or shame. It's a thing in our culture to spend time watching other people live on our electronic devices and make calculations about our lives based on what we believe is true about someone else. We spend time looking up to someone successful, and the secret message we tell ourselves is we won't be *liked* until we are on their level. We need to be perfect.

Some of us didn't even know we *weren't* successful until we logged in.

In *The Social Dilemma*, Chamath Palihapitiya, the former vice president of Facebook growth, said, "We curate our lives around this perceived sense of perfection . . . and instead what it really is . . . is fake, brittled popularity."

Social media is great for some things. It can add value to our dreams. But we need to consistently evaluate how our social media intake is affecting us. Is it resulting in us being more motivated, passionate, and happy? Or is it allowing us to drift from our goals and start measuring ourselves against unfair standards? We have to refuse to let someone else's *grid* make us feel bad about our *life*.

> WE SPEND TIME LOOKING UP TO SOMEONE SUCCESSFUL, AND THE SECRET MESSAGE WE TELL OURSELVES IS WE WON'T BE *LIKED* UNTIL WE ARE ON THEIR LEVEL.

2. BE CAREFUL NOT TO SHAME OTHERS

What contributes to us shaming ourselves is that we often shame others. We judge others at a standard neither they *nor we* can live up to.

We think less of athletes when they lose a championship game.

We think less of a lawyer who just lost a case.

We think less of a waiter or waitress who got our order wrong.

We think less of a leader who can't shake an addiction.

We think less of an author with typos.

If we think rather negatively of others when they fall short, we will naturally play our own tapes of judgment for ourselves when we fall short.

If you want to be truly accepted for who you are and not what you do, you should show love and appreciation for others before they accomplish anything. You should hit up the friend who was furloughed or lost their job entirely and let them know how much they mean to you.

I'm not suggesting we lower our standards. I'm merely suggesting we give others the break we would all love to have, because by not doing so, we're actually sabotaging ourselves. We're subconsciously creating a cancerous standard that leaves us disappointed with others and ourselves. You have the ability to release shame off someone else, and when you do so, it actually contributes to removing shame off yourself as well.

I'm not a naturally empathetic person, but I've

worked hard to really understand how a person feels. However, I'm careful to not fake it. I don't tell someone I know how they feel if I really don't.

The following is something Brené Brown said in her TED Talk on shame. (I know I'm quoting her again, but she's my therapist I've never met. Brené, if you're reading this right now, you rock!) "If we're going to find our way back to each other, we have to understand and know empathy, because empathy's the antidote to shame. If you put shame in a petri dish, it needs three things to grow exponentially: secrecy, silence and judgment. If you put the same amount in a petri dish and douse it with empathy, it can't survive. The two most powerful words when we're in struggle: me too."[3]

When I'm trying to get shame off a friend, I'm looking for a way to get in the boat with them and look for ways where what they're feeling is synonymous with something I've felt in the past. If it's not there, I ask questions to gain more understanding. One of the rules of thumb I live by is this: *People who have failed have already beaten themselves up without me. They don't need my help feeling bad.*

When I stop beating up others in my head or out loud, I'm setting a precedent for how to treat myself when shame comes knocking on my door.

3. BE AWARE OF YOUR SELF-TALK

What have you been telling yourself lately? What tape have you been playing? What voice have you been replaying over and over? What negative statement have you been agreeing with lately?

Sometimes when I sit with dreamers, they make balancing statements they believe will make them less vulnerable and soften the blow in case I think their ideas are dumb. You know what they sound like:

I mean, it's my first draft.
I put this together late at night.
I recorded it on my laptop.
My guy still needs to make some edits, but . . .

Whenever I hear these self-deprecating statements, I often respond with: "You don't have to do that." Sometimes I have to say it to myself too.

When I use phrases like these, I'm attempting to allow something to enter the space that I perceive hasn't been there: compassion. It's nice when someone else gives it to us, but my suggestion is, *why wait for them?* Why not give compassion to yourself before someone else does?

The art of self-compassion is important when

dealing with shame. Spending years trying to get others to accept you before you accept yourself is a recipe for disaster. Self-compassion is not giving yourself excuses for why you failed. Self-compassion is an awareness that you're human when you fail.

Too many times we treat ourselves like robots that don't need rest, nutrition, relationships, or compassion. I'm only human, and you are too. So give yourself a break. Show yourself some compassion. Tell yourself that your identity isn't on the line with your next idea. You're going to be okay, and shame doesn't get to be the boss of your dreams.

As I entered into writing this fifth edition of *Chasing Failure*, I struggled with a lot of mind games. Ninety-five percent of its content is new, but I wondered if I'd fail my team, my agent, and my publisher.

Honestly, I tried finding a ghostwriter. *And I failed at that too.* A part of me wanted someone else to be responsible if this went bad. I wanted a scapegoat. I wanted someone else I could cast shame on in the event of failure.

> **SELF-COMPASSION IS NOT GIVING YOURSELF EXCUSES FOR WHY YOU FAILED. SELF-COMPASSION IS AN AWARENESS THAT YOU'RE HUMAN WHEN YOU FAIL.**

But at the end of the day, I concluded that my readers had to really hear from me.

I've watched too many students beat themselves up over one grade.

I've seen way too many moms feel boxed in by traditional roles that have kept them from trying anything new.

I've sat with way too many executives who were one decision away from leveling up but were too afraid to take the risk.

I know community activists who would make great politicians but can't get past the criticism that comes with the territory.

I've read manuscripts from authors you'll never know about because they couldn't get past a what-if-it-goes-bad feeling.

Falling short four times set me up to take a fifth shot I didn't want someone else shooting. I hope this latest edition is successful, but hey, I can't promise you won't find a typo or two.

KEY TAKEAWAY ▬▬▬▬▬▬▬▬▬▬

What contributes to our shaming ourselves is that we often shame others. We judge others at a standard neither they nor we can live up to. If you want to be truly accepted for who you are and not what you do, you should show love and appreciation for others before they accomplish anything. We should give others the break we would all love to have ourselves. Answer this question: Who will you celebrate this week?

SEVEN

50 SHADES OF *THEY*

> Let me never fall into the vulgar mistake
> of dreaming that I am persecuted
> whenever I am contradicted.
>
> —RALPH WALDO EMERSON

In the summer of 2011, I overheard my then girlfriend Amanda say to a friend that she thought it would be cool to get engaged and married on the same day. At the time, I wasn't exactly sure what all that meant, but I concluded that if I wanted it to be a surprise, I couldn't actually talk to her about it. Over the next two years, without her having a clue, I began planning a surprise wedding.

On the morning of June 7, 2013, I knelt down on one knee and proposed to my wife at the Westin Diplomat Hotel in Hollywood, Florida. After she had accepted my proposal, I began a new proposal saying, "Well, the real question isn't, 'Will you marry me?' But the real question is, 'Will you marry me, *today*?'" She was perplexed and confused by the second question, and before she could gather her thoughts, I opened up a lounge door that had one hundred of our family and friends standing with a huge sign that read, "TODAY!" From there, we brought in the wedding dress, a makeup artist, her favorite hair stylist, and everything she would need for us to get married that night!

I had the entire day filmed and documented because I knew the day would be so chaotic that we would want to have a video to remember everything. When I was planning a surprise wedding for my wife, I wasn't planning it to create a viral YouTube video. In fact, I was only able to secure a videographer for the wedding two weeks before the day. We were married for three months before the documentary was finalized. Then I simply uploaded it on my wife's YouTube account and put it on Facebook to share with my friends. The first day "The Surprise Wedding" got ten thousand views. I couldn't believe it got that many views in a day. Within a week it had thirty-six thousand views. After that the views tapered off for a month until we were featured on *Good Morning America* and *The Today Show*. After those spots were aired, the video hit over a million views within a week.

It was cool and odd at the same time. You'd think the goal of any YouTube video would be to get as many views as possible. I guess that's true of our video, but I really just wanted to do something special for Amanda.

What's interesting about having a video on YouTube with over a million views are all the comments from strangers. Of the million-plus people who have viewed the video from around the world, eleven thousand of them gave it a thumbs-up. They *liked* it.

But, last time I checked, as of 2020, 194 people have given it a thumbs-down. They *disliked* it.

Which group do you think I focused on more? The thumbs-down crew, for sure.

Here's the good news for us, though: Thumbs-down, dislikes, and negative comments can be channeled into grit and can help us chase failure and go after our dreams. Criticism is feedback from others on the areas in which we need to improve. It sucks. I think most of us like the idea of being perfect, so when criticism comes our way, it shatters that illusion and we find ourselves in the reality that other people can see we are not perfect. Criticism comes in all shapes and styles. It can be constructive, destructive, passive, kind, subtle, blunt, or downright cruel. It can come from a boss, a friend, a spouse, a child, a stranger, a coach, an enemy, an internet troll, you name it. No matter what form it comes in, we can always learn from criticism. And I've found that when people embrace criticism, they become more adventurous, successful, self-aware, and downright interesting.

We need both negative and positive feedback to accomplish our goals. But we struggle to deal with the negative feedback the most. To embrace criticism as a tool to help us chase failure, we need to evaluate, extricate, and employ.

EVALUATE

What's been said about you? And what are you going to do with it? Evaluating criticism means that you aren't taking all criticism you receive as absolute truth. You know yourself better than most people you interact with do. So most of their remarks on your performance in an area shouldn't make you question your identity and skills.

Measure criticism you receive against your identity, behavior, and performance. See if the criticism has validity. Sometimes we have trouble recognizing the validity of criticism in our own lives. One of the more palatable ways of evaluating criticism is by having what I've come to call a Life Committee. The three individuals who make up my Life Committee are basically my personal board of directors. We get together over the phone and help each other make decisions about the future. It's a safe place for getting constructive criticism and for them to speak validity into criticism I've received from people outside of the group. If you don't have something similar, call a friend or colleague and see if you can create a safe place for you to have a mutually beneficial relationship that helps you both to grow!

EXTRICATE

After we've decided that there's some validity to the criticism we've received, we need to extricate the helpful and beneficial from the feedback.

I'll never forget speaking at my first Fortune 500 company. I bought a new suit. I hired a photographer to come. It felt like the first day of kindergarten for a grown man. Don't worry, I played it cool . . . *kinda*.

Many things can throw a speaker off, and a false introduction is one of them.

"Today's speaker is known for pulling off 'The Surprise Wedding,' and his story has been featured on *Good Morning America*, *The Today Show*, and *Oprah*! Give it up for Ryan Leak, ladies and gentlemen."

It was *The Queen Latifah Show*. Not *Oprah*!

Trust me, you never want to step in front of a crowd who, before you say a word, has given you Oprah-level expectations. On the other hand, if I began my keynote by correcting the president of the company who invited me to come, well, that's not a great start either. I just had to slightly insert the story of my wife and me going on *The Queen Latifah Show* in my talk. Nevertheless, I made it through the event the best that I could.

What I love about doing events for larger companies is that they usually come with a larger level of accountability and feedback. The companies were gracious to send me feedback from their employees from my training session. There were quite a few kind comments from employees. And then there were the responses that stuck with me:

> Ryan was entertaining and his experiences inspiring. It would have been nice for his presentation to focus more on the audience and how it could take steps to embrace risks and failure.

While Ryan's story was fun and interesting, I would love to hear from a speaker in the future that is "humbly inspiring" and more closely aligned, perhaps, with the work we do.

It took me a week to accept these, but the individuals had good points. I should have done more homework. While I was momentarily discouraged by the feedback, I decided that I was going to extricate the good from the bad. What I took from these comments, rather than a personal attack, was that I needed to be more aware of my audience and their context when I spoke, and that in doing so I would better align myself with the audience, making them feel comfortable and included. I needed to make my presentations more about the audience than about me.

When we extricate the beneficial from the discouraging, we make it more about sharpening our skillsets and less about fixing our personalities.

EMPLOY

Once we have evaluated and extricated the beneficial information from criticism, we can employ what we've learned by turning the criticism into actionable steps that will help us grow in our skills and abilities. The criticism I received from the Fortune 500 company guided me to know how I could improve my speaking. Guess what happened when I changed my presentation? It made me a better speaker. After the next event I spoke at, I didn't get that same feedback; I got different feedback and kept growing.

When we take criticism and turn it into action, we put ourselves in a position to be our best selves. When we actively seek out constructive criticism because we know it makes us better, that is when we are successfully chasing failure. Employing techniques we learn from criticism rather than ignoring them or taking them too personally will take us to the next level.

Contrary to popular belief, I don't believe we should be our own worst critics. Sometimes we criticize ourselves first as a defense mechanism so it doesn't hurt as bad when others do it. It's like when someone makes fun of themselves before anyone else can. But when we do that, it's like getting punched twice for no reason. People can have their opinions, but if I'm going to get jumped, I don't want to *help them* beat me up. A practice we should master is never saying to ourselves what we wouldn't say to someone we love. When the conversations about our dreams center around perfection, that's a toxic conversation we're having in our heads. But when the conversation about our dreams centers around giving our very best to it, that's healthy. Your goal isn't always to be the best, but to give your best.

Don't fall for the trap of trying to avoid criticism. You want criticism. You need criticism. It's how you get better. You can't have success without criticism. And if you can't have success without criticism, then what's so bad about failure with criticism? The way I see it, you're going to have criticism no matter which direction you go.

The method of evaluating, extricating, and employing in order to embrace criticism looks nice on paper with all its alliteration, but it is really difficult to implement. I know so many people who have analysis paralysis when it comes to putting themselves out there, and they sometimes have more fear of criticism than they do of actually failing.

YOU CAN'T HAVE SUCCESS WITHOUT CRITICISM.

Criticism often feels like rejection. And we are hard-wired to hate rejection.

The scary thing about rejection is that it clashes with our very human infatuation with being liked. The human part of us wants to be accepted and feel as if we're a part of a group or tribe. The Association for Psychological Science suggests that our quest for acceptance comes from our need for survival. It's been this way for a while.

In ancient times, developing allies was how you protected your land and family from enemies. Growing your tribe was strategic and was often done through marriage. Tribal life was normal and gave humans a sense of acceptance. Today, people are constantly searching for a tribe where they belong but are often faced with rejection.

Jia Jiang, speaker and author, had what most people would consider success. He was employed by a Fortune 500 company, making six figures, and living in a big house with a baby on the way. But what he really wanted was to be an independent entrepreneur. He built a habit-gamification app that ultimately failed after his pitch to a major investor was rejected. This particular rejection sent him in the opposite direction most go in. Instead of giving up, Jia decided to search out rejection and document his journey for one hundred days. He recorded himself making all types of crazy requests to people and companies. The result of that journey was his book *Rejection Proof: How I Beat Fear and Became Invincible Through 100 Days of Rejection.*[1]

One day Jia asked a friend for one hundred dollars. Another time, he asked for a burger refill (I guess that's where you just re-up on a second burger for no cost), then he asked to plant flowers in a stranger's backyard, and he asked a Starbucks employee if he could be a Starbucks greeter. He overcame his fear of rejection and learned he could turn a no into a yes by simply not running away from rejection. He has since coined the phrase *rejection therapy*, which basically means the more we lean into rejection, the more we can learn from it.

In his TED Talk, he said, "In my research, I found that people who really change the world, who change the way we live and the way we think, are the people who were met with initial and often violent rejections."[2] Rejection makes us stronger, and it allows us to chase bigger opportunities. Jia discovered that simply asking for what you want can open up possibilities where you expect to find roadblocks. He learned that he could achieve his life dreams by asking.

I've had my fair share of rejection. As a public speaker, you're pretty much asking for it. I remember the first time someone from TED Talks reached out about a potential opportunity to do an event for them. They had me pitch a few ideas, but I was rejected. I had to take it on the chin and keep moving. While being featured by TED has literally made some people's careers take off, I couldn't let that rejection define me or determine my abilities to communicate. I had to view it as another opportunity to keep working on my craft.

Whether writing a book, pitching a business idea to investors, trying out for a team, or interviewing for a new role, we all have opportunities to be rejected. Can you imagine living a rejection-free life where you were never told no? That wouldn't be good for you or me. We need to flip rejection on its head. Instead of saying rejection keeps us from opportunities, we need to see possible rejection as an opportunity.

When facing criticism and rejection, some have recommended going with the *don't-care-about-what-people-think-about-you* plan. The problem with that plan, though, is that it requires you to stop being human. Embracing criticism doesn't mean becoming emotionally impenetrable to what people think about you. It means you know *what to do with* what people think about you. Why we fear criticism so much rests on one vitally important question: Who are *they*?

You know, the proverbial *they* who exist in your

mind who have all these negative things to say about you. Who are they? What are their names?

Are *they* people you went to middle school with?
Are *they* your neighbors?
Are *they* prospective clients?
Are *they* your coworkers?
Are *they* your parents?
Are *they* your siblings you've been compared to your whole life?
Are *they* strangers on the internet you hope respond to your post?
Are *they* social influencers?

Who's the group of people you're hoping to get the best reaction from? Who's the group of people you're hoping to impress? Now let me ask you this: Why? Why is it important to impress *them* specifically? I've found that the more I actually say *their* names out loud, the more embarrassed I am that I even want to impress *them* in the first place.

There used to be a specific group of people I wanted to impress with my speaking abilities. That was, until one day I got on a stage and realized *they weren't even in the room.*

Half of my speaking events are in corporate settings,

and the other half are in church settings. In the church world, there can be a temptation to give messages that are impressive to other pastors. So initially, pastors were my *they* when I was speaking in church settings. The problem is, I don't write church messages for pastors. I write church messages for people who are trying to know God, make a change, and figure out what their purpose in life is. It took me a couple of years too long to realize I had the wrong *they* steering what I was doing.

Once I shifted my focus to *the right they*, the people I was supposed to have been writing messages for from the beginning began giving me feedback that helped me become a much better communicator. Once you've got the correct *they*, you can start embracing criticism and sharpen your skillset so you can be the most successful failure chaser ever.

Something phenomenal can happen in our lives when we learn how to embrace criticism and rejection. We don't all perform on the world's biggest stages, but we all have people who give us their opinions about who we should be and how we should live. Something powerful happens when we channel negative opinions into positive energy.

You can wait for someone to give you feedback to improve your skills, or you can beat them to the punch by putting yourself in a position to get better by inviting feedback into your life and opening yourself up to the potential for rejection. When you open yourself up and stop fearing criticism and rejection, you set yourself up for daily wins that will help you get to where you want to be.

KEY TAKEAWAY

Identify your *they*, and embrace everything you can learn from criticism and rejection.

EIGHT

ALL I DO IS WIN

Ideas are powerful, but not as
powerful as your habits.

—SCOTT HAGAN

I set my alarm for 6:00 a.m. to write this chapter. And here's how the rest of the morning went.

6:01 a.m.: Get out of bed.
6:08 a.m.: Get to my office, which is twenty feet away from my bed.
6:09 a.m.: Sit down at my desk and open up my laptop.

6:10 a.m.: I think I should start the day off by drinking a bottle of water.

6:12 a.m.: Get to the kitchen and decide I should probably take vitamin D too.

6:15 a.m.: Go back to the office. (*Why did it take me three minutes to take vitamin D? I'm not sure.*)

6:17 a.m.: As I open up this manuscript, I think I should probably put God first, so I read some scripture . . . which leads me to open up the Bible app on my phone . . . which leads me to the unread text messages I have from the night before.

6:45 a.m.: I'm ready to start writing, but I'm not comfortable in my office because I can feel a cold draft breathing down my neck from the A/C unit.

6:50 a.m.: I'm in my closet trying to pick out a sweatshirt, but I can't just pick any sweatshirt because, in the middle of a pandemic, I always have to be Zoom ready.

6:59 a.m.: Back in the office and it's showtime.

7:00 a.m.: My kids wake up and want to know what "we" are doing today.

7:10 a.m.: I sneak out of my office, which my kids believe is their playroom, and I turn our entertainment room into my office.

7:20 a.m.: Entertainment room has a pretty large entertaining electronic device hanging on the wall. I figure I could put on some music via YouTube to put me in the writing mood.

7:25 a.m.: NBA playoff highlights appear as a suggestion. I figure clicking on that would get my brain going, right?

7:26 a.m.: An alert comes on my TV saying it needs to be updated and that it'll take fifteen minutes.

7:41 a.m.: NBA playoff highlights clicked.

7:55 a.m.: I pull a quote from some lady that could be used for this chapter.

8:00 a.m.: I then research said lady for twenty-seven minutes only to find out Twitter hates her, and if I quoted her in this book, you'd probably burn it.

8:27 a.m.: I'm hungry, but I'm doing intermittent fasting and can't eat until noon. I go to the kitchen to get a greens drink. My kids are there and my oldest asks me for pancakes. I then convince him to go present that request to his mother.

8:45 a.m.: My best friend calls me about the NBA playoff game I just watched highlights of.

9:00 a.m.: I get an alert on my phone that I have a Zoom call with a client in an hour, and I still need to prepare for it. I debate for twenty minutes on whether or not I should try to knock out some of this chapter in the time I have left or if I should prepare for the Zoom call. I decide to work on the book.

9:20 a.m.: My wife swings by and says, "Are you gonna wear *that* on your Zoom call?" (I picked the wrong sweatshirt.) She follows that up with, "Can we do lunch today?"

Three and half hours into the time I set aside to just write, I had a chapter title and one quote from a lady I couldn't use. The reality is, I procrastinated writing this chapter . . . on *procrastination*.

For authors, we sometimes call it writer's block. But what about when you have podcaster's block?

And filmmaker's block?
And speaker's block?
And athlete's block?
And leader's block?
And designer's block?

Sometimes it's a blank canvas, a blinking cursor, a list of names and phone numbers that serve as a block between us and our goals. I wonder if *block* is the best word to even describe our status in procrastination. Underneath that block is really just fear. I've found my delays are not because I've run out of ideas, but that often the ideas I've had weren't ones I thought anyone else would like. When you're stuck, you have to ask yourself why you're *really* stuck.

At some point all the books you've read, podcasts you've listened to, and information you've absorbed have to turn into an *action plan*. A dream without a plan is just a hope. If you've counted the cost of what it takes to get from where you are to where you want to be, you then have to develop your own action plan of what you're going to do next.

This is why we have to-do lists.

But if you're anything like me, you've written out a to-do list only to just stare at it sometimes. How many times have you done the hard work of making a plan and setting a goal and simply got sidetracked? We could call it getting distracted, but if we're honest, we *welcome distractions* when we're afraid to fail. I'd rather watch Netflix than attempt to do something that can make me look or feel unaccomplished.

A DREAM WITHOUT A PLAN IS JUST A HOPE.

Have you ever spent an hour just staring at a blinking cursor because you had no idea how to start *one* email? It's as though we believe English professors at Yale are receiving all our emails. But I get it. It's hard mustering up the courage to write something to a person or group of people we believe has their stuff together more than we do. There are lots of *ifs* we struggle with.

- *What if it sucks?*
- *What if nobody likes it?*
- *What if nobody likes me?*
- *What if nobody will follow me?*
- *What if I can't raise the capital?*

I have a friend who told me about a recent project he created to help people get rid of their excuses entitled *Shut the IF Up*. I was intrigued. It made me put my own justifications for lack of forward progression under the microscope.

So how do we create an action plan that works? We do so by answering these three questions:

1. What needs to be done *this month* to move toward my overall goal?
2. What should be done *this week* to move toward my overall goal?
3. What can I do *today* about my overall goal?

If you were to do a quick search on New Year's resolutions, you would find multiple sources, across many years, stating that only about 9 percent of people successfully reach their goals. And about 80 percent of people give up by the second week in February. One of the reasons the failure rate is so high is because of the way we set our goals—by making them something to accomplish during a whole year. You're really setting yourself up to fail on that one. Look at what you need to accomplish over the next month and divide it by four to get your weekly to-do list. From there you'll realize what you can pull off in just one day. Daily goals are much more practical and measurable than yearly goals.

Between speaking, writing, coaching, and podcasting, there's never a week when I don't have at least one project to work on, but there's one principle, one mantra, and one habit I've put in place that has helped me get over my own procrastination and get things done: get one win every day. I am laser focused on winning each day of the week. I can't worry about tomorrow, but I can give my best today. And by trying to win every day, I get an opportunity to fail and learn from those along the way. Focusing on daily goals and wins turns into daily habits.

GET ONE WIN EVERY DAY.

I love what science-fiction writer Octavia Butler

said in her book *Bloodchild and Other Stories*: "First forget inspiration. Habit is more dependable. Habit will sustain you whether you're inspired or not. Habit will help you finish and polish your stories. Inspiration won't. Habit is persistence in practice."[1]

I believe the daily habit of short-term winning helps you get through the days when you fail. Even if you fail, you will have created a habit that will sustain you if you feel like moving on to something else. Even though I failed making an NBA roster, my training habits from the experience of trying out have helped me win daily as I stay in shape and become an even better basketball player.

Losing twenty pounds might be what's needed, but no one loses twenty pounds at one time. They lose it one pound at a time. No author finishes a book in one sitting. Authors finish books one paragraph and one chapter at a time. Achieving an audacious goal is already daunting; you might as well break your very large goal into small-size pieces that are actually attainable.

One of the life hacks that has helped me the most is starting off each week by creating a list of thirty to forty items to check off on a to-do list. When I wake up in the morning, I simply try to knock one item off the list. I only need to get one win. What I've learned about daily wins is they turn into weekly wins and monthly wins.

When I first began thinking about making podcasts, I had no idea what was involved in putting one together. So I went to my buddy Zach, who knows a lot about audio engineering, and said, "Hey, man, I'm thinking about starting a podcast." He replied, "I'm in." I responded, "Well, that was quick." I expected him to at least think about it for a second. He then replied, "When do we start?"

I had told him I was *thinking* about starting a podcast. I didn't say I was *planning on* doing anything. I was still in the creation and innovation stage of the idea, but nothing about a podcast had made its way to my sacred weekly to-do list.

When do we start? I was wondering *can* we start?

So I had to change my tune and my mindset. I then asked him, "What does it take to start a podcast?" And then I allowed him to give me homework. First, he said I needed to figure out the format.

- *Would I have guests?*
- *Would I or would someone else be the host?*
- *What's the podcast about?*
- *What platform do I want to distribute the podcast through?*

I didn't have answers to any of those questions, but I had a few thoughts. He told me to get answers to those questions and then my next step was to get a quality microphone.

On my to-do list for that week were these items:

• Decide if you want to have guests.
• If no guests, then decide if you need a host.
• Consider Peter Reeves (a dear friend) to be your host. Call him.
• Order microphone off Amazon.
• Practice an episode.

So the next day, I decided on having no guests during season one of that particular podcast and that I'd call my friend Peter to see if he would consider being a host. I was able to get three wins in about thirty minutes. The following week, Peter and I practiced an episode and it just wasn't good.

I sent the recording to Zach, the newly appointed podcast editor, and he gave us technical adjustments we could make to improve the podcast.

Peter and I were doing practice recordings utilizing Zoom as the media hub for all we were recording. During one practice recording, I made a random decision to make this podcast both video and audio. I then asked Zach what it would take to make that happen. He sent me homework, and I added it to the to-do list. During the years, we've recorded so many bad episodes that have been edited and then canned because I didn't feel good about them. But it was those bad episodes that helped me make better episodes, and it still happens to this day.

I love this perspective, which is often attributed to Dale Carnegie: "Inaction breeds doubt and fear. Action breeds confidence and courage. If you want to conquer fear, do not sit at home and think about it. Go out and get busy."

Most of us don't want to fully commit to a dream project until it's perfect. But what's perfect on day one? A good friend of mine, Nick Nilson, once said, "People admire perfection, but they can't relate to it." Imperfection actually breeds connection. I've shifted my daily mindset from trying to make my content perfect to trying to make my content better. When we fall for the trap of believing it has to be perfect, we have sold out to the notion we have something to prove.

You have nothing to prove.

To your parents.

To your friends.

To your boss.

To your colleagues.

To your teacher who didn't believe in you.

To your former coach.

To your ex.

I'll say it again for the people in the back: You have nothing to prove! And you have everything to improve. My goal each day is to have one thing on my to-do list that gives me the opportunity to improve something.

Out of the thirty to forty items on my to-do list, five to ten of them require a large amount of mental energy. Some weeks I try to tackle those earlier in the week to get the hard stuff out of the way, but I often get distracted. Earlier I described how my mornings sometimes go. I might find myself at the end of the day with no wins on the hard stuff, but I'll pick one or two easier items I can knock out that will give me a win for the day. The small win for the day gives me confidence to go for a bigger win tomorrow.

YOU HAVE NOTHING TO PROVE. AND YOU HAVE EVERYTHING TO IMPROVE.

I've literally created such a habit of winning that when I fail, I sometimes don't even realize it. For example, I completely missed the deadline for the manuscript of this book. But I was still winning every day with this project by getting small wins. Some days I finished a chapter. Other days I finished coming up with one chapter title.

If you're easily distracted like me, the Do Not Disturb mode on your electronic devices will aid you in getting daily wins. Push notifications are the death of focus.

You can win once a day. You might lose some days, but you'll get more daily wins than daily failures. And your daily wins can turn into weekly and monthly wins.

I know you may not feel like moving past your fears, but just win today.

I know people's opinions are intimidating, but don't live for other people's opinion of you.

I know you might not come from money, but you can win today without money.

I know you might not have the network that others do, but you can win today without a network.

I know you may not have a bunch of people who believe in you, but if you believe in yourself, you can still win today.

I know you might have one person who told you that you'd never be able to accomplish your goal, but they never told you that you couldn't win today.

Don't worry about winning some day. Focus on winning today. You want to create a habit of consistency. Extraordinary people do *consistently* what ordinary people do *occasionally*.

Nebraska Furniture Mart CEO Irv Blumkin calls every single employee on their birthday. They've got

EXTRAORDINARY PEOPLE DO *CONSISTENTLY* WHAT ORDINARY PEOPLE DO *OCCASIONALLY.*

upwards of 2,800 employees. Most people would consider themselves lucky if their manager remembers their birthday, let alone getting a phone call from the CEO. But he has a list provided to him every day and makes the calls personally because he is an extraordinary leader.

In a 2012 interview with Techonomy Media, Jack Dorsey, CEO of Twitter and Square, explained his daily routine for a season where he was juggling a full-time role at both companies. To get everything done, Jack said he would put in an eight-hour day at each company, *every day*. He did this for only a limited time as he shifted most of his focus and energy to Square, but when he was pulling double duty, he was doing sixteen-hour workdays, Monday through Friday.

Jack pulled this off by giving a theme to his days. Each weekday was dedicated to a particular area of the business at both companies. Here's what his themed week looked like:

MONDAY: Management and running the company
TUESDAY: Product
WEDNESDAY: Marketing and communications growth

THURSDAY: Developers and partnerships

FRIDAY: Company culture and recruiting

Jack said this method of theming his days helped him stay focused even when he was often interrupted.[2]

Imagine if you gave your day a theme and just aimed to win in that particular area. If you want to pull off something extraordinary, you have to have extraordinary habits. You may or may not run two companies. But you have a life, and in order to pursue your dream, you're going to need some time management to fit failure chasing into your schedule. So maybe pull a Jack Dorsey and break up your week thematically. Monday, Wednesday, Friday is for studying; Tuesday, Thursday is for chasing failure. Find what works for your schedule, and do it.

As I mentioned earlier, *the first key habit to chasing failure successfully is finding a win every day.* When we only make big resolutions and our to-do lists are filled with tasks like "end world hunger," then we will find ourselves discouraged and content with letting failure find us. But when we break down what we need to fulfill our dreams into small, actionable steps, then we are one phone call, one errand, one paragraph closer to realizing our wildest dreams. My advice to you: write stuff down. Use a calendar, use a to-do list—these tools are your friends.

WHEN WE BREAK DOWN WHAT WE NEED TO FULFILL OUR DREAMS INTO SMALL, ACTIONABLE STEPS, THEN WE ARE ONE PHONE CALL, ONE ERRAND, ONE PARAGRAPH CLOSER TO REALIZING OUR WILDEST DREAMS.

Writing a book for me is very lonely. It's like having a meeting with nine versions of myself in a room, and they're all arguing about the book.

One of them is a perfectionist. He's captain grammar, and he's annoying.

One of them is the clarity police. He says, "I get what you're trying to say, but you can say it better."

One of them questions everything. He says, "That's kind of true, but I can think of about fourteen circumstances where that's not factual at all." He pokes holes in everything.

One of them always has his glass half-full and thinks happy thoughts.

One of them is thinking about the next book.

Another one of them is hungry.

Another one of them wants to play with his kids.

And one of them just wants to watch NBA highlights instead of writing.

One of them is the leader, and he just keeps telling all the *Ryans* . . . just win today.

KEY TAKEAWAY

Decide what you need to accomplish this month and this week to create a practical to-do list. Pick one item today and get it done. Just win today.

NINE

FRIENDS, DON'T FAIL ME NOW

> If you hang out with chickens, you're
> going to cluck and if you hang out
> with eagles, you're going to fly.
>
> —STEVE MARABOLI

I love the art of storytelling. I get to do that through writing books, speaking, and podcasting, but the avenue I dreamed of telling stories growing up was through film. It's what got me into video production in high school and college. I got a business degree, but my last elective I had in college was a script-writing class. Had I taken that class earlier in my college career,

I probably would have switched to film school. I loved it that much. That's what led me to start a small motion graphics and video production company right out of college.

When I was first starting out, I did everything for shoots. I set up all the cameras, lighting, and audio. Sometimes I'd even act in the projects if necessary. I was a one-man band.

Anybody with any sort of film aspirations has explored the possibilities of moving to Hollywood, and I found myself in that boat in my early twenties. My sister-in-law's uncle (I'm not sure if that means he's actually related to me or not—the jury is still out on that) has been a first assistant director on quite a few major feature films. So I was given the opportunity to spend a little time with him in Southern California for an afternoon to learn more about the movie business.

I learned a lot about the inner workings of how a movie comes to be.

I had sent him one of the projects I worked on of which I was most proud to get his perspective on how it could be better and wondered if he thought I had potential to make it in Hollywood. He had a few observations, but only one I remember.

He said, "Your stuff is good, but it's just you, man. The difference between my projects and yours is that, at the end of your project, the only name that comes up for the closing credits is yours. At the end of mine, there's hundreds. The one thing I would submit to you is that perhaps you're doing too much by yourself." He was so right.

Most of us walk out of movies when the closing credits come on the screen, but those names reveal a major part of the story of how the movie became a movie at all. I once read that the movies *Titanic* and *The Lord of the Rings: The Return of the King* both listed about two thousand names in their closing credits. I didn't count them, but I'll take their word on it. My projects had one.

His advice led me to start hiring contract employees to be able to handle many more projects than could be completed on my own. What I want to encourage you with is this: your goals have a higher chance of success if you involve others in the process. Get in the habit of including other people in your dreaming process. Invite others to chase failure with you.

When it comes to pulling off what feels impossible, I often think of addicts. Addicts often have a desire to change but don't often

YOUR GOALS HAVE A HIGHER CHANCE OF SUCCESS IF YOU INVOLVE OTHERS IN THE PROCESS.

have all the tools to pull it off. In 1938, Bill Wilson created Alcoholics Anonymous (AA), a twelve-step model Wilson wrote out while sharing ideas he had been developing through his experience with and view of alcoholism. He highlighted the positive effects experienced when people struggling with alcoholism shared their stories with one another. To achieve something that felt impossible, Wilson saw they would have more success if they involved others to join them on the journey.[1]

I believe the same is true for you and what you want to accomplish. When you invite others to be a part of your goals, I believe you benefit from these five opportunities:

I. AN OPPORTUNITY TO HAVE ACCOUNTABILITY

The executive coaching practice I have has been built primarily with one ingredient: accountability. So many executives have untapped potential because they work in an environment where no one challenges them to be better. My company puts together accountability plans to help executives become who they want to be.

I'm such an accountability ambassador that I'd actually tell you your goal is likely doomed without an accountability plan. You can have all the resources and even the *it factor* to pull off something audacious. But you need accountability for your weakest moment and your darkest hour.

Here's something all of us have to come to grips with: We're not very good at keeping ourselves accountable. We need help. And we don't have to make accountability harder than it needs to be. To set up accountability, all you need is a clear goal and a willingness to let others help you achieve it.

In a 2018 *Forbes* article titled "Three Steps to Overcoming Resistance," Stacey Hanke wrote that the American Society of Training and Development (ASTD) discovered you have a 65 percent chance of completing a goal if you tell someone else. (Like when I told Kobe and friends I was going to try out for the NBA.) Your chances of success increase up to 95 percent if you have a specific accountability appointment with someone.[2] An accountability appointment differs from a deadline in that you've become so strategic about your plans that you've put dates on the calendar where you're going to connect with someone about your goals.

> WE'RE NOT VERY GOOD AT KEEPING OURSELVES ACCOUNTABLE. WE NEED HELP.

I do this with our clients all the time. They have the choice of weekly, biweekly, or monthly meetings depending on what they want to accomplish, but every meeting serves as accountability to keep the ball moving forward.

Accountability can be formal or informal. I have clients who I keep accountable in a formal and professional manner. But I also have friends who I keep accountable on a much less structured and informal basis, and they do the same for me.

My wife's best friend, Vasti, called us one Friday to ask us if we would call her every night at 10:00 p.m. Monday through Friday to see if she had worked out. Her plan was to begin a series of workouts every day starting first thing Monday morning.

We accepted that new role as her accountability partner on a new journey of hers, but it didn't go how she thought it was going to go.

I called her *Sunday* afternoon and said, "Let's go."

She said, "Let's go where?"

I responded, "Turn off that Celtics game, lace up them Adidas, and let's get after it. I'm not calling you on Monday. Tomorrow's not promised, young lady! You might not get a Monday. Now let's go!"

Accountability can be annoying. But it works.

I have another friend, Larry, who kept telling me

for months about a podcast he was going to start on marriage. He had ideas for names, but he had apprehensions about the whole process. So whenever he'd send me an idea for a name for the podcast, I'd respond with a screenshot of the GoDaddy.com link showing the URL for his idea was available for $11.99. Building a website is intimidating. *Buying the URL for a website just requires a few clicks.* (Side note: This is low-hanging fruit for progress. If your goal would eventually require a website, buy the URL. It's an easy win, and you need as many of those as you can get.)

Larry bought the URL for his idea and had some excitement around it for a couple of weeks, but he has seven children and is one of the top executives at his company. He's already got a full plate for sure, but he kept telling me he was going to get it done. So I made a deal with him. I gave him a calendar date three months out and told him that he and his wife needed to record a podcast by that date or he'd have to buy me a brand-new camera drone that cost around six hundred dollars. He agreed to the terms. *I was happy because this was a bet where I had nothing to lose.*

Literally on the last day of the bet he and his wife were in the garage of their home recording their first episode, and I couldn't have been prouder of them for taking that first step. I was sad about the drone, though.

As a person's friend, I have a vested interest in helping them succeed, so keeping someone accountable is an easy switch for me to turn on. The person who keeps me accountable on many areas of my business(es) and life is my friend James. He asks great questions that leave little room for excuses on moving forward.

Who in your life would be a prime candidate to keep you accountable for where you want to go?

While you think about that, let me offer you two friends who make great accountability partners and will never forget to remind you of what you need to do next: Alexa and Siri. If you own a smartphone, you can actually tell it to remind you of anything you want, and it will do so without fail.

2. AN OPPORTUNITY TO *GET* ASSISTANCE

Whenever you tell someone else what you want to accomplish, two things automatically happen. First, people will ask you how it's been going whenever they see you. Second, the people you tell will think of you whenever they encounter others they believe can help you.

This is why I'm a major advocate for sharing your goals with family and friends. I told so many people I was chasing failure with the NBA that I was continually being asked how it was going.

"Hey, did you try out for a team yet? You said you were chasing failure, right?"

The more answers I didn't have for them, the more motivated I became to figure it out. You want to make it embarrassingly difficult for you to give up on your goal.

I then had friends who wanted to connect me with cinematographers for the documentary. And those cinematographers knew graphic designers who could help me with the website.

YOU WANT TO MAKE IT EMBARRASSINGLY DIFFICULT FOR YOU TO GIVE UP ON YOUR GOAL.

And those graphic designers knew people who could help with email campaigns.

The point is, it's okay to ask for help. In fact, you need to. Some people you ask help from may not be able to help or may not want to, and that's okay too. I'm still waiting for some people to text me back or respond to an email where I requested their assistance, but whether or not I hear from them will not keep me from moving forward. You should never go without assistance simply because you weren't willing to ask or receive it.

By sharing your goals and vision with others, you're also risking something: someone you love could think less of you. Someone could think it's a dumb idea. I know it's scary, but you actually need those moments now to prepare you for much worse later. By *not* sharing your goals and vision with others, you're still risking something: not knowing who could have helped you succeed.

3. AN OPPORTUNITY TO *GIVE* ASSISTANCE

Sharing your goals is engaging in the power of networking. Networking can sometimes get a negative reputation of a group of individuals entering a space with hidden agendas. But it doesn't have to be that way. I'm consistently looking for win-win relationships, not just where I get something from them but also where there's something of value I can give.

Wayne Baker, a sociologist at the University of Michigan, explained, "If we create networks with the sole intention of *getting something*, we won't succeed. We can't *pursue* the benefits of networks; the benefits ensue from investments in meaningful activities and relationships."[3]

It's easy to want to take withdrawals from others.

But it's a lot more meaningful to want to make investments in others. Sharing your goals gives you the opportunity to do the latter.

The idea you have could produce jobs for those who need them.

The idea you have could spark another idea for someone else.

Here's a rule of thumb to live by: Whenever you find yourself stuck on your goals, help somebody else with theirs. If you're losing, help somebody else win.

Starting a podcast was intimidating. Starting a second podcast shortly after the first was even more intimidating because the elephant in the room was that I hadn't really mastered podcasting on the first one. What I've learned about myself is if I wait for everything to be perfect, I'll never do it. Podcasting has been learning on the fly for me, but in the process of sharing it with others, I've had several opportunities to tell people what *not* to do when starting a podcast.

HERE'S A RULE OF THUMB TO LIVE BY: WHENEVER YOU FIND YOURSELF STUCK ON YOUR GOALS, HELP SOMEBODY ELSE WITH THEIRS.

The notes you take on the good, bad, and ugly of chasing failure are all helpful for yourself and others.

4. AN OPPORTUNITY TO LEARN WHAT
TO DO *WHEN YOU FAIL OTHERS*

When you involve other people, there will be moments when you let them down. You'll drop a ball. You'll disappoint a client. A meeting with someone a friend or family member connected you with will go bad because you weren't as prepared as you thought you were, causing your friend or family member to look bad. These moments can make you want to give up altogether, but you shouldn't.

When I was eighteen years old, my first client hired me to produce an annual recap video for their Christmas party. I filmed everything I needed to ahead of time and even went to the CEO's office a couple of times to show him drafts of the video. He was very excited.

Editing videos requires rendering and processing to export the video into a file that can be played. Unfortunately, when I hit the final render of the video, my computer processing system (this was in 2004) didn't render the video in time for the party, and what could be rendered and played was a choppy version of what I had created. It flopped at the Christmas party, and I was embarrassed, and my client was disappointed. The only thing I could do in that moment was own up to my mistake and apologize.

When you make mistakes, be sure to take owner-ship for them. If you can learn this sooner than later, you won't keep failing. When it comes to repairing relationships, I have spent thousands of hours trying to get people to use words like . . .

- *I'm sorry.*
- *My bad.*
- *This one's on me.*
- *I should have been more prepared.*
- *I was wrong.*
- *Forgive me.*

Those words are difficult to use because of our pride. Pride is so dangerous for our goals. The old saying "Pride goes before the fall" comes from a verse found in Scripture written by one of the most successful men to ever live, Solomon. But the saying has been slightly flawed in how it's quoted. Here's what it actually says: "Pride goes before *destruction*, a haughty spirit before a fall" (Proverbs 16:18, emphasis added).

It's a slight difference in wording, but a massive dif-ference in meaning. Pride coming before a fall sounds trivial, like a slap on the wrist.

But it's a lot worse than that. Solomon said "destruc-tion." If you were packing your bags to go on vacation to a destination where I knew a nuclear bomb was going to be detonated that would *destroy* that city, I would do everything in my power to warn you not to go there. *Consider this your warning with pride.*

WHEN YOU DROP A BALL OR FALL SHORT ON A PROMISE YOU'VE MADE, OWN IT.

It will ruin every relationship you have. When you drop a ball or fall short on a promise you've made, own it. It's hard to accomplish anything meaningful without engaging with other people. Though you will fail people along your journey, if you're willing to own up to your mistakes, it will serve you in the long run. What's worse than any mistake you can make is not having the ability to admit it when you have made a mistake.

You don't have to beat yourself up, but you do need to apologize and try to do better next time.

5. AN OPPORTUNITY TO LEARN WHAT TO DO *WHEN OTHERS FAIL YOU*

News flash: people will fail us. We know that already. But we don't always know what to do when that happens. Might I suggest you treat them how you'd like to be treated? I'd be willing to guess that you'd want to be given grace when you mess up. The greater the failure, the greater the grace required.

Arguably one of the most influential figures during the information revolution was a guy named Tom Watson Jr., who served as CEO of IBM from 1956 to 1971. During his time at IBM, there was a young executive on his team who failed miserably. He made some bad decisions that cost IBM several million dollars. One day, after one particularly bad failure, he was summoned to Watson's office, with the full expectation to be fired. As he entered the office, the young executive said, "I suppose after that set of mistakes you will want to fire me." Watson reportedly replied, "Not at all, young man, we have just spent a couple of million dollars educating you."[4]

Giving grace to someone else who has failed comes down to your perspective on failure altogether. Sometimes the working relationship needs to come to an end and the personal relationship needs to continue. But regardless of how well you handle it when people drop the ball, you need to know that people failing you is actually really good for you.

It can be scary to let someone else in on your dream. It can be hard to let go of control and let other people help you and hold you accountable. It can be hard to have to tell someone you were rejected or you failed or you were criticized. It feels easier and safer to just keep those things to ourselves. But that is the number one way to not grow.

If you don't let people into your dreams, you will remain stagnant and unsuccessful. Neither will you have anyone to share the exciting news with, because no one would have known your journey and how hard you've worked. To chase failure successfully, you need supportive failure chasers around you. You will have a better chance of cornering failure that way.

So don't let your name be the only one on the screen when the credits roll.

KEY TAKEAWAY

The chances of completing your goal increase dramatically if you share your goal with someone. Who's a prime candidate in your life to hold you accountable with regard to what you want to accomplish in the future?

TEN

JUST DO IT SCARED

A ship is safe in harbor, but that's
not what ships are built for.

—JOHN A. SHEDD

I'm a pastor's kid, the son of Reverend Emmanuel
Conway Leak. What that means is I grew up in an
environment where I had to be ready for a variety of
unknown duties at any moment. When your family
runs a nonprofit business, you live at the mercy of vol-
unteers showing up on time and ready to serve in their
roles. But in the event they don't show up, it's next man
or woman up.

At our small church growing up, we had a choir director who also played the organ. He was typically on time, but we certainly had a few Sundays when he showed up after the service had begun. He was also in charge of making sure the church had a drummer. And the drummer also had a time or two when he was a no-show.

I'll never forget one of those occurrences when the choir director was trying to lead the congregation in music without a drummer. This was a season in my life when I wore a three-piece suit to church as a nine-year-old. I looked up at my mother and told her, "I can do it." She said, "Do what?" I said, "I can play the drums." I had never played the drums in my life, but I had seen my brother play and thought it was so easy a caveman could do it. (I absolutely could not play drums. I was a preadolescent who knew no limits.)

My mother took off my jacket in what felt like slow motion to me, and like a mother eagle sending her young out of the nest to fly for the first time, she sent me down the aisle toward the front. The congregation could see me making my way to the drum set, and they knew I had never played the drums before. In my mind, I wasn't at a church. I was in an arena heading toward the scorer's table, and the crowd was going wild because I was about to be in the game.

I sat at the drum set and picked up the sticks. And right as I was about to clang a cymbal for the first time, the drummer showed up. I thank God he did, because if he hadn't, it would have been a catastrophe.

I wish I could tell you I wasn't scared, but the truth is I was shaking in my loafers. Since then, I've been thrown in the deep end without a life jacket many times. And sometimes, I jumped without being pushed. There's so much to learn in the deep end. It's probably wiser to learn to swim in the shallow end, but where's the fun in that?

Entrepreneur Sara Blakely said, "One of the most common questions I get to this day is, 'When you started Spanx, what was your business plan?' Here's my secret: I didn't have one! No, really, I didn't. I had never even taken a business class. Because I had no idea how it was supposed to be done, I kept it as simple as possible. I focused on 3 things: Make it, sell it, build awareness. I made the product, sold it to as many stores as I could and spent the rest of my time building excitement and awareness. Then I would repeat the cycle. That's it!"[1]

Sometimes you just have to go for it. One of my favorite quotes is by author Glennon Doyle: "If you can't beat fear, just do it scared."

As a public speaker, I get to do about 120 events a

year. I have the opportunity to reach thousands on a weekly basis. As an executive coach, I get to train about twelve thousand leaders a year. I'm constantly creating content for courses, workshops, conferences, church services, corporate keynotes, new book projects, and, currently, two podcasts. I wish I could tell you I never get nervous and I don't sweat it, but that's not true. *I just do it scared.*

> **I WISH I COULD TELL YOU I NEVER GET NERVOUS AND I DON'T SWEAT IT, BUT THAT'S NOT TRUE. *I JUST DO IT SCARED.***

Being in front of thousands of people a year, I'm asked this question most often: "Do you ever get nervous?"

"When do I *not* get nervous?" is a better question. I'm always nervous. I always have a part of me that thinks, *This is going to go awful.* But I've learned to do it scared.

There are four core principles I've adopted that have helped me deal with fear:

I. STAY READY

Growing up in a church environment where I had to be ready to sing, speak, or play an instrument has served me well in my adult life. It instilled in me a mentality to stay ready so I don't have to get ready.

In my early twenties I wanted to be a speaker but hadn't been given many opportunities to do that yet. So I began writing messages and keeping them on my phone. If I had a thought or an idea, I would flesh it out fully as if I was being given an opportunity to do what I love. I would practice the messages in the shower on a regular basis. (Ironically, there are messages I speak today that I wrote a decade ago.)

I've got this buddy named Kent who's a pastor in Chicago. He's notorious for helping leaders grow by putting them in positions to step up without warning. I was visiting his church one time during their first of two services that day, when he saw me in the crowd. At the end of the service, he asked me to speak at the next service that started in twenty minutes. Though I was nervous, I said yes because I was also ready.

The first time I spoke to a professional sports team, I was given a day's notice. The first time I presented a proposal to my largest client to date, I was given four days' notice. I wore a nice suit, but the proposal had quite a few grammatical errors.

There's always an event around the corner for me. When I'm working with a church or a company, I always ask them what the touchdown is for them. I want the messages I give to be about them and them winning. But because of that, I end up writing forty to fifty messages a year. I'm constantly creating content that could fail completely. Unfortunately and fortunately, I often don't have the luxury of getting over the nerves and the fears before the events, so I just do them scared.

One of my mentors introduced me to a tool called the Enneagram, which highlights nine different personality types and how they affect the way people see the world. I found it fascinating, and it produced one of the most meaningful conversations my wife and I have ever had. It helped us understand each other and the world around us tremendously. I immediately started diving into all things Enneagram, and slowly but surely I began to weave it into my executive coaching practice.

One day I was sitting in an office with one of my CEO clients and telling him about how I thought the Enneagram could help him personally and how it could help his organization. He said, "Great. I want you to do a workshop on that *Monday* for the whole company." (It was Friday.)

Workshop? Bro, I read some books on this thing. I never said workshop.

"It's going to be great. I'll catch you Monday," he concluded.

Insert me pulling two all-nighters to get ready because I absolutely was not ready for a workshop. Keynote expectations are a well-polished one-hour presentation. Workshop expectations are four to six courses with key learnings, PowerPoint slides, group exercises, and a workbook. I was ready for the former. I was not ready for the latter.

Then came Monday and fifty people walked into the room. The first guy I see said, "We're learning about the ennea-*what* today?" "Enneagram," I replied. The PowerPoint slides had a few grammatical errors. Some of the slides were even out of order. The workbook was a hot mess. I was completely embarrassed and felt like I bombed.

The reality was, the majority of people in the room had never heard of the Enneagram, and they didn't know the slides were out of order because they didn't know what the order should have been in the first place. I clicked fast through the slides with spelling errors. While I was embarrassed, I now had a new workshop I could improve upon.

Since then, I have been certified as an official Enneagram coach. I've done plenty of those workshops now, but I never stop tweaking them. There's always something to improve.

I've tried controlling my nerves, but I usually don't

get the chance to do that fully before it's showtime. I'm better at controlling my readiness. When I sit with my friends who are in the NBA, they constantly talk about staying ready. Some of my friends play forty minutes a game, and some never know if they'll play at all. Both have to stay ready.

You should start writing chapters *scared* now.

You should start putting together proposals *scared* now.

You should start designing concepts *scared* now.

You should start recording *scared* now.

You should start working on that website *scared* now. (You can do a basic one on Wix.com for free.)

YOU SHOULD START PREPARING NOW FOR THE OPPORTUNITY YOU WANT IN THE FUTURE, BECAUSE YOU NEVER KNOW WHEN YOU'LL BE THROWN INTO THE DEEP END.

You should go to that networking event that has all of those people you think are smarter than you because they have graduate degrees and you don't. Yeah, go scared and intimidated and have the time of your life anyway. You should start preparing now for the opportunity you want in the future, because you never know when you'll be thrown into the deep end.

2. REMAIN TEACHABLE

Some things you learn from others. Some things you have to experience on your own.

One time I was asked to speak to a group of college students in a leadership development program. I had this exercise I had done with leaders in the past that worked really well that I sort of copied-and-pasted into this event. This exercise was simple in ideation, but rather complicated once fleshed out.

How it worked was I would have leaders share what they thought was broken within their organization. I'd write their answers on a whiteboard and then talk about ownership and accountability. I created sort of an *aha* moment that the problems that exist in an organization are the responsibility of the leaders and no one else. It was a basic ownership talk with a splash of trickery.

When I went to do it with these students, I had them text their answers to me anonymously, and they were brutally honest about what they thought was wrong with the program. One guy texted me about one of the leaders of the program he thought should be fired. *I didn't write that one on the whiteboard.*

I felt the talk going south the more anonymous texts I received. It was getting more and more awkward because the leaders of the program were in the room with the students, and the students could own some of the issues. Instead of an aha moment for student leaders, I simply provided an open-ended bashing session of the program and its actual leaders.

The head of the program asked to talk with me afterward, and I went into his office thinking it would be a neutral conversation about what was put on the board. That was false. He gracefully told me that, as a guest, you don't go opening cans of worms and then leave. They felt my presentation for the day was rather inappropriate, and his leadership team was not prepared to get bashed in what was supposed to be a time of growth and development.

I was young and didn't know any better. But he gracefully gave me a hard lesson I wish I could have learned at someone else's expense.

I spoke at my alma mater a couple of years after I graduated. I still had friends who attended the university who were freshmen when I was a senior, and it was good to see all of them. When I got up to speak, I greeted the students with, "It's good to see *old* friends." There was a gasp in the audience, as apparently I had offended my *current* friends who thought I considered them long forgotten. If you offend an audience at the beginning, it's hard to rebound. It's not impossible, but it's not good. Needless to say, that message didn't go over too well.

I was then invited to give a pregame pep talk to the basketball team I had played for years prior. The guys were happy to see me, and I was happy to get to see them play, but the speech I gave them before the game did not go over well with the coach.

I don't remember my exact wording in the speech, but I said something along the lines of *relationships matter more than education*. The coach, who was trying to get his players to go to class and do well in academics, just had his former All-American tell his current team that education isn't that big of a deal.

It was there that I learned the value of reading the room. Again, I was young and didn't know better. But there are only two ways to know better: your experience or the experience of others.

You will have moments when you'll quote the wrong person. Sometimes you'll laugh at something no one else thinks is funny. Sometimes you'll have days when you weren't sensitive to the moment. But all of those moments are designed to help you learn from them and grow. If you stay teachable, you don't have to let previous failures keep you from moving forward.

3. DO THE RIGHT THING FOR
THE RIGHT REASON

This principle is what I consider to be my *failure insurance*. I fall short of my goals. I make mistakes in presentations. I write typos. But in the process of failing, I do my best to treat people well and do all of my work with a high level of integrity. I'm consistently asking myself: *What's the right thing to do?* I'm annoyingly and constantly checking my motives.

This is good for me and also good for you because when you check your motives often, it's less likely that other people will question them. We've all been around someone with a hidden agenda, and even though we don't know what it is, we get a feeling about that person we certainly wouldn't want someone to have about us.

I was taught early on in business that it's a dog-eat-dog world. I was taught that only the strong survive, and the only way to get ahead in this world is to do whatever it takes to knock out your competition. I was taught if you want to climb the corporate ladder, pull someone else off. Contrary to popular belief, I believe you can actually get ahead by being kind, treating people well, and doing the right thing for the right reason.

This doesn't mean you're a pushover, but it does

mean you sleep well at night knowing you've done right by yourself and others. I'm all for competition, but if I have to sacrifice my integrity to win in business, then I've lost what is most dear. There's nothing worse than a gifted person who is not respected by his or her colleagues, close friends, and loved ones.

THERE'S NOTHING WORSE THAN A GIFTED PERSON WHO IS NOT RESPECTED BY HIS OR HER COLLEAGUES, CLOSE FRIENDS, AND LOVED ONES.

When you do the right thing for the right reason, people will give you grace and the benefit of the doubt when you fail because they trust who you are more than what you do.

Because I allow clients to steer my content, I'm often writing new material, which gives me the opportunity to fail almost weekly. There are pros and cons to this business model. One of the cons is my chances for failure are higher than if I was presenting a familiar message more frequently.

I once had this event where I would be speaking to nearly a million people on XM radio. My friend leading the event gave me the choice to present a familiar talk or a new talk that was on brand with where they were in that season of their organization. It was better for me to do a familiar talk, but it was better for them if I gave a new talk in sync with the messages they were already trying to get across.

I did the message that was brand-new, and it was underwhelming. I felt like I couldn't get in the zone, even though I was confident I had done the right thing. Afterward, my friend asked me how I thought it went. I responded, "It was okay, but it certainly wasn't my best. Still, I did feel like it was needed. I'm always toiling between what I want and what is needed, and tonight I chose what I thought was needed."

He responded, "Not many speakers are willing to do that, and that's exactly why you'll be invited back."

I wish that was how all of my flops ended, but they don't. But whether I win, lose, or draw, I rest well knowing I've done the right thing for the right reason.

4. CONSISTENTLY ENGAGE IN ACTIVITIES THAT INTIMIDATE YOU

When it comes to fighting a fear of failing, you have to frequently move toward activities that intimidate you. Like jumping out of an airplane over and over, it gets a little less nerve-racking the more you do it.

Can I tell you who the most impressive people in the world are to me? It's *door-to-door salespeople.*

I have mad respect for telemarketers, too, but getting hung up on is not the same level as getting an actual door shut in your face. When they knock on my door, I'm uncomfortable for the both of us. Do you know the amount of courage it takes to knock on a stranger's door and try to sell them pest control in sixty seconds or less? Do you know the amount of mental stability one must have to ring the door of someone they've never met, hoping to get them to buy cologne or a vacuum cleaner? They have no earthly idea whose door they're knocking on. They could be knocking on the door of a murderer for all they know.

But the reason I find their craft so impressive is because they are putting themselves in the prime position to build resilience. I can only imagine the number and types of rejections they've encountered in their careers. It's only because they're willing to fail that they even have a chance at succeeding.

Perhaps the most intimidating thing I've had to face over and over again in my career is talking about money with clients, especially when providing services to a nonprofit organization. The range of budgets organizations have for speakers and coaches is broad. I never want to overcharge someone, but I also don't want to underestimate the value I can add to an event or a team. I've lost gigs quoting beyond a budget. I've lost money quoting way below their budget. Neither felt good. But I've kept engaging in the uncomfortable conversations, and over the years I've gotten a little cozier with discussing my value propositions.

Email marketing, technology, building websites, social media, leadership, finances, public opinion, and all the other things that hold dreamers back are things that get a little less scary when we just keep jumping out of the airplane.

Those are my guiding principles for how I'm able to do things scared. What are yours? Mine may be helpful, but I encourage you to come up with some of your own to help you along the way when you fail. When we're able to build the habit of doing things scared, we are able to go further than we ever could in our comfort zone.

KEY TAKEAWAY

You can't always control your nerves, but you can always control your readiness. Answer this question: How can you prepare better for future opportunities?

ELEVEN

IF AT FIRST YOU DON'T
FAIL, TRY AGAIN

In a world that's changing really quickly,
the only strategy that is guaranteed
to fail is not taking risks.

—MARK ZUCKERBERG

When I think about my teenage years and where I spent
a considerable amount of my leisure time, I would have
to say I spent those years in a store called Blockbuster.
For the Gen Zers reading this, Blockbuster was a place
where you could rent movies or video games for a

couple of days at a time; and it was a weekly routine of mine to go to Blockbuster to borrow entertainment for the weekend for my family or friends. There were intense moments in my home over someone forgetting to return a video game, VHS, or DVD before being charged a late fee. In those days, I could see no entertainment future without Blockbuster.

According to a 2010 *Washington Post* article, at its peak Blockbuster ran 9,904 stores worldwide with revenue topping $5.9 billion a year.[1] Their secret sauce was those dang late fees that brought in roughly half a billion dollars a year. (I've contributed at least five hundred dollars to Blockbuster late fees in my life cycle. Shame on me.)

In the late 1990s, an internet upstart named Netflix had the idea of giving people an opportunity to subscribe to a DVD-by-mail service where a person would no longer have to leave home to pick up their entertainment. And the idea was that a person would pay a flat monthly fee instead of paying for each rental.

This new subscription service's popularity exploded, and executives from Netflix flew down to Texas in 2000 to make an offer to sell Netflix to Blockbuster for $50 million. Reportedly, the idea was that Netflix would join forces with Blockbuster and help them launch their own online and DVD-by-mail service. But the CEO of Blockbuster, John Antioco, reportedly laughed Netflix out of the office, seeing that the new subscription service was losing money at the time.[2]

However, Netflix would have the last laugh. Because according to *Forbes*, as of April 2020, Netflix was valued at $194 billion, while Blockbuster closed its last store in 2013 after filing for bankruptcy in 2010.[3]

It would have been a risk for Blockbuster to buy Netflix at the time, but it would have been a risk worth taking. And I know what you're thinking.

Hindsight is 20/20, Ryan. Of course, it's easy to look at the past and see what someone should have done.

And you're right. I don't want you to be the story of what you should have done. What hindsight teaches you and me is that in the event we succeed, we can't be afraid to keep taking risks. The temptation when you make a lot of money is being so afraid of losing it that you do not take any risks. The temptation when you gain a lot of followers is being afraid to say anything that might lead to losing followers. Success can actually have a way of making us even more afraid to fail.

SUCCESS CAN ACTUALLY HAVE A WAY OF MAKING US EVEN MORE AFRAID TO FAIL.

There are three types of risk I want

to encourage you to continue taking in the event that you succeed.

I. STRATEGIC RISKS

According to the US Census population projections released in March 2018, the nation will become "minority white" in 2045. During that year, whites will comprise 49.7 percent of the population in contrast to 24.6 percent for Hispanics, 13.1 percent for blacks, 7.9 percent for Asians, and 3.8 percent for multiracial populations.[4] Which means, for you and me, our future will be a lot more diverse than our past, and even our present. The world will continue to change, but the question is, will we?

Does what you want to accomplish reflect where culture is or where culture is going?

The number one action I spent the majority of my coaching sessions helping clients take during the 2020 pandemic was simple: *pivoting*. Those sessions felt like counseling sessions, where I endeavored to get them to divorce outdated patterns and blueprints and embrace new technologies and strategies. Change is difficult for a lot of people, but it's necessary. It's always going to be difficult to reach new goals with old habits.

We have to be willing to take some limited strategic risks and try new approaches if we want to set ourselves up for success in the future.

On December 13, 2013, Parkwood Entertainment President and Chief Executive Officer Beyoncé Knowles ventured out to do something unprecedented in the music industry by releasing a self-titled album without fanfare, prior promotions, or advance marketing. This was also Beyoncé's first time moving forward with a release without assistance from her father or any other outside management company.

But Beyoncé had a vision for something different. She told Lee Anne Callahan-Longo, Parkwood's general manager, "I want my fans to be able to listen to it first without any filters, and I want it to be a visual album that has a video for every song, and I don't want the album to leak."[5]

In an AutoPlay video on Beyoncé's Facebook account and a one-word message on her Instagram account, the message simply read: "Surprise!"

Beyoncé was scared about how fans might respond, but breaking records, the album quickly jumped to number five in the UK and number one at home in the US.[6]

It was an unconventional and risky strategy, but it further added to the fierceness of her legacy. The music industry has changed tremendously between 2000 and 2020, and it most likely will continue to change. Artists, musicians, and labels all have to reevaluate their strategies and be willing to fail in the process.

In his MasterClass on leadership, Bob Iger recalled the day he called Steve Jobs to pitch the idea of Disney buying Pixar. Iger remembered being "incredibly nervous." When Bob told Steve he had a crazy idea, Steve said, "Tell me more about your crazy idea." And Bob said, "I've been thinking about the need to fix Disney animation. I don't have any great solutions. The one idea that keeps coming back to me is the notion of buying Pixar." He continued with, "You've got the great talent and the great technology, we've got the great legacy that is Disney."[7]

Before Steve responded to Bob, there was a momentary pause. If you have ever pitched or proposed anything live, you know that a pause at the end of your pitch feels like years, not seconds. Bob recalls getting sweatier by the minute. But finally Steve responded, "It's not the craziest idea I've ever heard."

A couple of days later, Iger flew to meet Jobs in Northern California. They convened in a boardroom with a whiteboard and began making a pros-and-cons list for Disney buying Pixar. "There were about three pros and about twenty cons," Iger said. In the meeting, Bob told Steve, "Well, I guess this isn't going to happen."

And Steve replied, "Why do you conclude that?" Bob said, "Well, look at the board: the cons outweigh the pros to such an extreme." It seemed like it was a non-starter to Bob. And Steve said, "No, I'm looking at these pros and I think they far outweigh the cons."

"Steve's mind was just incredible in that he had an ability to kind of cut through it all and really look at the essence of something," Iger continued in the MasterClass. He said that Steve concluded, "The pros here were that both Pixar and Disney would thrive and would be better off together than separate."

Bob Iger was willing to make a phone call that altered the destiny of Disney Animation. Disney bought Pixar for a little more than $7 billion in 2006. Within the first fourteen years from when Disney first bought Pixar, the animation studio's films have grossed a combined $14.4 billion at box offices around the world, according to data from Comscore.[8]

All that couldn't have happened if Iger hadn't been willing to make a scary phone call and ask for what he wanted. That strategic risk really paid off.

When I speak at an event, if I'm in a mood to chase failure, I have the option of engaging with the audience where I allow them to yell stuff out loud. I tested this one time while speaking on fear to a group of middle schoolers. I decided I wanted to try starting off the message by allowing said middle schoolers to scream out one by one their biggest fears. (If you're nervous to hear what they said, you should be.)

I asked the first kid, "Hey, man, what's your name?"

"Trevor," he replied.

"Trevor, what a great name. What's your biggest fear?"

"Um . . . heights," he responded.

"Heights? I totally get that. Who's your friend next to you?"

"Alex."

"Alex, what's your biggest fear?" I asked.

He said, "Sharks."

The students were having fun. They were engaged. This felt like a good idea at the time, right up until the moment I pointed out another adolescent young female in the audience and said, "Hey, what's your name?"

"Siri," she said.

I said, "Siri, can you tell me what your biggest fear is?"

It felt like slow motion entered the space. The room got quiet. She paused for what felt like an hour. And then she told me and a room full of people what her biggest fear was: *her grandfather dying.*

She answered the question truthfully and honestly, and it wasn't her fault that I had set her up to reveal that to a few hundred of her peers. Needless to say, recovering from that did not go well. But I learned from that experience. I took a risk and utilized a strategy I don't typically use to learn what can work and what absolutely cannot work. Developing content for written or verbal communication is an art form. I'm always trying out new stories, jokes, or illustrations because I never want to get so comfortable that I can't pivot when I need to.

In the event you get good at *what* you want to accomplish, remain flexible on *how* you can do it better.

2. FINANCIAL RISKS

If we were to examine some of the top companies in the world, we'd find they've all committed a considerable amount of money to one thing that is vital for their future success: research and development (R&D). According to *Forbes*, covering the fiscal year ending on June 30, 2018, here are the big spenders in research and development:

- Amazon took the first-place trophy for the second year in a row with $22.6 billion spent on R&D.
- Alphabet, Google's parent company, came in second place with $16.2 billion.

- Samsung spent $15.3 billion.
- Intel spent $13.1 billion.
- Microsoft spent $12.3 billion.
- Apple spent $11.6 billion.[9]

If we were to add up the research and development budgets of the top one thousand public companies in 2018, we'd find that they collectively spent a whopping $782 billion on R&D in 2018.

These companies aren't successful because they had a few good ideas. They're successful because they set aside a portion of their budget to investigate ideas.

An example of that is when Amazon's Fire phone was introduced and released in 2014 but was discontinued the following year. Three-dimensional face-scanning technology was one of the phone's big selling points but was ultimately viewed by critics as a gimmick. On the surface it seemed like a critical and commercial failure costing Amazon billions, but that's not Amazon founder Jeff Bezos's take on it at all.

In Amazon's 2019 annual letter to shareholders, Bezos wrote, "As a company grows, *everything* needs to scale, including the size of your failed experiments. If the size of your failures isn't growing, you're not going to be inventing at a size that can actually move the needle. Amazon will be experimenting at the right scale for a company of our size if we occasionally have multibillion-dollar failures. Of course, we won't undertake such experiments cavalierly. We will work hard to make them good bets, but not all good bets will ultimately pay out."[10]

Bezos then went on to cite the infamous Fire phone failure saying, "Development of the Fire phone and Echo was started around the same time. While the Fire phone was a failure, we were able to take our learnings (as well as the developers) and accelerate our efforts building Echo and Alexa."[11]

As of 2019, customers have purchased over one hundred million Alexa-enabled devices. The lessons you learn from losses can be transferred to future wins. Sometimes a company has to spend billions to make billions.

But what about you? What are you willing to spend to get better after you've already had success?

I think everyone should have a personal exploratory budget within their means that is set aside to research and develop the potential of future endeavors.

I have a successful client who works in finance who had a side

WHAT ARE YOU WILLING TO SPEND TO GET BETTER AFTER YOU'VE ALREADY HAD SUCCESS?

hustle idea for trading video games digitally. Initially, I thought the idea had a lot of merit and could be rather lucrative, but my first apprehension was wondering how he could make it *legal*. My advice to him was to reach out to a lawyer to research what it would take to pull off the idea. And that cost money.

Sometimes financial risk means investing in a coach who can mentor you and come alongside you to challenge your own status quo. Success can make you comfortable and lazy. One of the two most underrated investments you can make is the one you make in yourself. The second underrated investment you can make is the one you make in others, which leads us to the third type of risk you should take in the event you succeed.

3. PEOPLE RISKS

When successful people arrive at their destination, they often have one of two perspectives when evaluating the people around them, and especially the up-and-coming. Most choose the perspective that believes:

- *They need to work as hard as I did to get where I am.*
- *They need to grind.*

- *They need to hustle.*
- *They need to do the homework.*
- *They need to sleep in their car.*
- *They need to work on four hours of sleep.*
- *They need to invest what I invested.*

Maybe they need to do some or all of these things. Maybe *not*.

There's also the alternative perspective, which believes you worked hard, you grinded, you did the homework, you slept in your car, you worked on four hours of sleep, and you invested what you needed to invest in . . . so they don't have to because you want to give them the head start you never got.

I heard Rick Warren tell a story at a leadership conference once that blew me away. His book *The Purpose Driven Life* was on the *New York Times* Best Sellers list for over ninety weeks and reportedly sold thirty-two million copies within its first decade (by 2012). Warren said he had the idea for his bestselling book in his late twenties, but it didn't get published until his late forties. As he was telling this story, he said, "You want to know what that makes me feel like doing now . . . ?"

It felt like everyone in the audience knew where he was going with this story. We thought it was going to be a lesson on *maturity* or *waiting* or *trusting the process*, but he pivoted in the opposite direction.

He said, "It makes me want to find a twenty-seven-year-old right now with an idea and invest in them now."

Yes, people who are following after you need to learn hard lessons, but they don't have to be the same lessons you learned. You worked hard so they could have tall shoulders to stand on.

I'm a product of people taking chances on me week after week. I've been hired by so many event planners who could have had more qualified speakers, but they gave me the opportunity anyway. I have had too many let's-see-how-this-goes moments to count. The scales have been tipped in my favor often, and it simply makes me want to do the same for others. I've taken quite a few risks on people who have failed me miserably. But I have to continue to believe the best in people because there are moments when I've blown it and clients have graciously given me the benefit of the doubt. How can I not give that to others?

One of my clients who has locations all over America has always done their best to give felons a second chance. The laws are different for each state, but in their Minnesota location, the Huber Law allows prisoners, under certain guidelines, the privilege of leaving the jail during necessary and reasonable hours for a short list of reasons, primarily including employment. My client works with local institutions to employ felons, knowing it's risky.

At their Georgia location, they partner with Atlanta Transitional Center, which prepares adult male felons who are nearing the end of their incarceration to assume responsible citizenship. When I asked my client about this second-chance program they've committed to within their company, he said, "Has it gone bad a few times? Absolutely. But do we have more great testimonies than bad ones? You bet."

If there's someone in your world you've counted out, maybe you should count them in.

In the event that you find yourself doing a lot of winning, don't forget to stop and look around for someone you can give a chance to. Give them the opportunity you wished you'd had sooner.

KEY TAKEAWAY

Success in the future will require risk-taking and pivoting. Answer these questions: What risk have you been reluctant to take? What would it look like for you to move on it soon?

TWELVE

DON'T WAIT FOR MONDAY

Never be afraid to try something new.
Remember, amateurs built the ark;
professionals built the *Titanic*.

—UNKNOWN

I have another confession: I love food.

I love all kinds of food. I love fast food. I love slow food. I love appetizers. I love the main course. I really love ice cream. What I don't always love is how I feel after I eat all of the above.

It's hard to eat healthy.

And healthy people, they are so judgmental, right?

I remember when I started getting Naked Greens drinks and a healthy person said, "Ew. There's a lot of sugar in those." To which I thought, *More than a strawberry shake from McDonald's?*

One time, after I had begun drinking more water instead of Kool-Aid, a healthy person looked at my water and said, "Well, it's not *alkaline* water. Spring water is dirty water."

And picking up that organic chicken was a decision I was pretty proud of until my plant-based-diet friends came over to the house and grabbed grass from my yard on their way in as an appetizer.

The overall diet of my twenties could be described as a roller coaster of eating healthy for about two weeks and then looking for every excuse to get a cheat meal.

My birthday.
My wife's birthday.
Our anniversary.
My sons' birthdays.
My mom's birthday.
My brothers' birthdays.
Easter.
Fourth of July.
Christmas.
Thanksgiving.

Halloween.

Black History Month.

Okay, so maybe I looked for not only cheat meals but cheat weeks and months as well. I have a more consistent rhythm now, but when my body was managing a zigzag diet, my mind was managing what it would take to really change. I lived with a mentality that I would change first thing Monday morning.

It's like we're prone to have Monday resolutions. Monday feels like the natural time and day to get a fresh start on anything new. But in the event you're reading this book and it's Tuesday, it's still a great day to start something new. Wednesday is just as good a day as Monday to start chasing failure. Did you know you can actually give yourself a fresh start right now? Don't wait for Monday.

Resolutions allow us to create plans for future behavior, but tomorrow's plans are no match for what you could pull off today. We all have great intentions of becoming greater later. We all have great intentions to work out more next year, to eat healthier after the holidays, and to build up our savings accounts once we get our tax returns. It's like we believe that our circumstances will change once we're in a better position to change our circumstances. Historically, however, that notion's success rate is rather low.

The only option you and I have is to simply become today who we intend to be tomorrow.

RESOLUTIONS ALLOW US TO CREATE PLANS FOR FUTURE BEHAVIOR, BUT TOMORROW'S PLANS ARE NO MATCH FOR WHAT YOU COULD PULL OFF TODAY.

I've often heard success can really be measured by how many people go to your funeral, but I don't think that's true. I think the better measurement would be what people say at your funeral.

In 2015, I lost a thirty-one-year-old friend, Liz Shepherd, to cancer. This is the part where I'm supposed to say it was really sad. And it was—but it was actually more inspirational than sad. We miss her like crazy, but she lived life in such a way that her legacy has impacted thousands upon thousands of people. My wife and I attended her memorial service at a church in South Dallas, and it was packed full of people who all had the same story. Every person who talked about Liz had a similar story about how she had gone the extra mile for them in some way or another. I had one of my own.

People say you know who your real friends are on the day when you're moving. We all hate moving our own stuff, let alone somebody else's stuff.

On a day when I had five or six friends say they would show up to help me move, they all ended up having lame excuses for being a no-show. Liz was available to help, but she didn't have a vehicle. I was in a moving truck at the new place, and my car was at my old place, so I told Liz that if she could somehow get to my old place (which was three miles from where she lived), then she could grab a couple of boxes and bring my car to me.

I didn't expect her to actually figure all that out—especially when it started to rain.

But Liz put on a light rain jacket and decided to *run* three miles in the rain to my old apartment. She showed up at my new place an hour later with my car filled with boxes.

At this memorial service, I learned that I wasn't the only one Liz had made an impact on by going the extra mile (and in my specific case . . . three miles).

Liz's husband had the courage to get up and talk about her at the service, and I'll never forget what he said. He read a Bible verse that says, "Love is patient, love is kind. It does not envy. It does not boast. It is not proud. It does not dishonor others, it is not self-seeking. It is not easily angered. It keeps no record of wrongs." And then he said, "You can actually replace the word *love* with *Liz*, and it would still all be true."

He then recited it like this:

Liz is patient.
Liz is kind.
Liz does not envy.
Liz does not boast.
Liz is not proud.
Liz does not dishonor others. *Liz* is not
    self-seeking.
Liz is not easily angered.
Liz keeps no record of wrongs.

He continued, "You know how at memorial services people usually make up crap about their loved ones to make everybody feel better? This isn't one of those memorial services. If anything, we have understated who Liz is and was." He was right.

It's funny, because people left that service saying, "I want someone to be able to replace my name in a Bible verse." And I responded, "Then you're going to have to start being kind, because I won't lie for you at your memorial service."

We all want people to say we were kind, patient, generous, and amazing, but what we should want more is for it to actually be true.

I had a lot of plans for 2020. I planned to travel

to thirty different cities and speak to over two hundred thousand people. And then the coronavirus changed all my plans, as I'm sure it did yours. At first, I thought COVID-19 would be similar to the Ebola scare. I thought it would blow over after a few weeks, but then everything started to get canceled. I found myself resigning from my visions of what I wanted to accomplish in 2020.

And then I woke myself up and realized today is the day to make moves. Sure, it might look different, and there will probably be more face masks involved and certainly more Zoom calls, but there is no time like the present to fulfill my purpose and achieve my dreams.

I began chasing failure via Zoom calls. I began recording talks for digital platforms. Ironically, I was able to speak to thousands more people digitally than I could have in person. COVID-19 actually presented me with an opportunity to speak in multiple places at once. And I was able to speak into the fear, anxiety, and paralysis a lot of people were experiencing during the pandemic. I found that a lot of people had the same tendency I had: to put their dreams on hold until the circumstances were just right.

But the reality for you is circumstances are never going to be just right for going after your dreams. Life tries its best to get in the way. We have day jobs and kids and bills and busy schedules. And I relate. But dream chasing should be included in that list. Dreams are what motivate us and get us up in the morning, and they make all our other responsibilities more exciting in the process. Don't wait until Monday to start factoring in your dream (unless you are reading this on a Monday, of course).

While fighting cancer, Erwin McManus wrote a book called *The Last Arrow: Save Nothing for the Next Life.* In it, he wrote, "The tragedy of a life that is never fully lived is not solely the loss of that one life. The tragedy is the endless number of lives that would have been forever changed if we had chosen to live differently."[1]

THE REALITY FOR YOU IS CIRCUMSTANCES ARE NEVER GOING TO BE JUST RIGHT FOR GOING AFTER YOUR DREAMS.

Hey, the world needs you fully alive. The version of you that is fearless could change a whole community. So *what* are you waiting for to make a move? You're smart. You can figure out the answer to that question. It could be valid or an excuse. But you can overcome whatever it is.

But here's the question you may never know the answer to: *Who's waiting on you?* Somebody is on the other side of your dream whose life will be radically different if you pull it off. And I'd hate for you never to meet them because you never tried. Would you be so afraid to fail if you knew your failure would set someone else up to succeed?

A single dad needs your book.

An addict needs your practice.

An overwhelmed mom needs a moment to laugh during your comedy show.

A felon needs a second chance working at the business you could start.

Food deserts need your healthy but affordable grocery store.

A soul needs your church.

A student needs your YouTube channel.

A future CEO needs your podcast.

A family who has experienced injustice needs your law degree.

Whatever it is you'd do . . . if you knew you couldn't fail . . . go for it. There are endless Mondays but only one today. Have I set you up to fail? I certainly hope so.

KEY TAKEAWAY ▰▰▰▰▰▰▰▰▰▰▰

Become today who you intend to be tomorrow. Answer this question: What are you actually waiting for to start changing your life?

CONCLUSION

Befriending Failure

Once you have the framework for realizing what dreams to pursue and the game plan to start working toward your aspirations, you, my friend, are ready to start chasing failure. And in the process, you'll find successes, you'll find innovations, you'll find fulfillment, you'll find challenges. You'll find friendships. And you'll find your dreams evolving.

Instead of playing in the NBA, I now have the privilege of working with NBA players and executives.

Chasing failure landed me in NBA locker rooms for a skill I possess off the court. Running up and down that court in Phoenix, I never could have imagined the opportunities that one event would produce in the future. To be able to come alongside NBA players now, long past my ability to play professional basketball, is one of the many things I feel privileged to do on a daily basis. I can make a difference in the lives of people on or off the court. You just never know where leaning into failure might take you.

Your dreams are worth chasing. And yes, you will experience failure along the way, but that has to stop being a deal breaker. Stop failing by default. Chase it down, look failure in the eye, greet it if you are feeling friendly, and befriend it. You'll be hanging out with it a lot as you chase your dreams. If you get an opportunity to fail, consider yourself lucky. Take out a pen and pad, and get ready to take copious notes on every flop, misfire, and failure. Let failure remind you that you are getting closer and closer every day to achieving what you once thought was impossible. Find your sweet spot, figure out your game plan, and go after your dreams.

So one more time, I must ask you:

What would you do if you knew you couldn't fail?

I certainly hope the world finds out.

5 . . . 4 . . . 3 . . . 2 . . . 1 . . .

ACKNOWLEDGMENTS

To my wife and children, thank you for the sacrifices you make that allow me to be me. Thanks for letting me work late. Thank you for being so understanding of what I believe God has called me to do.

To my brothers, thank you for letting me learn from your experiences and giving me a blueprint on how to succeed.

To my mother, thank you for bringing me to the planet and being my biggest fan.

To the Committee, and my dearest friends, I should write a book about all of you because you've been there for me regardless of my failures or successes, and I'll always remember that.

To James Wilson, thank you for consistently talking me into being a better human.

To Esther, and the whole Fedd Agency team, thank you for representing me and believing in this project enough for me to go for it a fifth time.

ACKNOWLEDGMENTS

To Damon, and the whole W Publishing team, thank you for partnering with me on this project and supporting me all the way through.

To all the churches and corporations that have me speak each and every year, thank you for giving me the opportunity to do what I love.

To all the people who work with the Ryan Leak Group, LLC, thank you for your help producing every post, video, podcast, graphic, PDF, message, and email that is created to inspire and help people move toward the person they were meant to be.

NOTES

CHAPTER 1: SETTING YOU UP TO FAIL

1. Po Bronson and Ashley Merryman, *Top Dog: The Science of Winning and Losing* (New York: Grand Central Publishing, 2013), 3–5.

CHAPTER 2: KOBE MADE ME DO IT

1. Kobe Bryant, *The Mamba Mentality: How I Play* (New York: Farrar, Straus and Giroux, 2018), 22.

CHAPTER 3: REFRAMING FAILURE

1. Paul Lazdowski, "7-Footers: 17-Percent Chance of Playing in NBA," *Boston Globe*, March 8, 2014, https://www.bostonglobe.com/metro/regionals/west/2014/03/09/footers-percent-chance-playing-nba/fNnbP8zybYfXZtsw0eYPDK/story.html.
2. "Former Hewlett-Packard CEO and New York Times Best-Selling Author Carly Fiorina on How to 'Find Your Way,'" *The ThriveTime Show*, https://www.thrivetimeshow.com/business-podcasts/former-hewlett-packard-ceo-carly-fiorina-on-how-to-find-your-way/.

CHAPTER 4: NEVER GIVE UP-*ISH*

1. Tamara Chapman, "Condoleezza Rice Interview: The Full Transcript," *University of Denver Magazine*, June 1, 2010, https://magazine-archive.du.edu/current-issue /condoleezza-rice-interview-the-full-transcript/.
2. Rob Bell, *Everything Is Spiritual* (New York: St. Martin's Publishing Group, 2020), 97–98.
3. Adam Green, "Lin-Manuel Miranda's Groundbreaking Hip-Hop Musical, *Hamilton*, Hits Broadway," *Vogue*, June 24, 2015, https://www.vogue.com/article /hamilton-hip-hop-musical-broadway.

CHAPTER 5: WHO *WANTS* TO BE A MILLIONAIRE

1. "Self-Publishing Grew 40 Percent in 2018, New Report Reveals," Bowker, October 15, 2019, http://www .bowker.com/news/2019/Self-Publishing-Grew-40 -Percent-in-2018-New-Report--Reveals.html.
2. Will Smith, "The Truth About Being Famous," YouTube, Nov. 26, 2018, https://www.youtube.com/watch?v= 0MvOvZWN23M.
3. Darren Rovell and Bobby Marks, "How Much the NBA's Biggest Stars Actually Earn," *ESPN*, September 19, 2017, https://www.espn.com/nba/story/_/id/20715128/nba -player-salaries-take-home-pay.
4. Rovell and Marks, "NBA's Biggest Stars."
5. Malcolm Gladwell, *Outliers: The Story of Success* (New York: Little, Brown, & Co., 2008), 35–68.
6. Mayo Clinic Staff, "Exercise: 7 Benefits of Regular Physical Activity," Mayo Clinic, May 11, 2019, https://www.mayoclinic.org/healthy-lifestyle/fitness /in-depth/exercise/art-20048389.

CHAPTER 6: SHAME *OFF* YOU

1. Brené Brown, "Listening to Shame," TED Talk, March 2012, https://www.ted.com/talks/brene_brown _listening_to_shame?language=en.
2. *The Social Dilemma*, film directed by Jeff Orlowski (Boulder, CO: Exposure Labs, 2020), https://www .netflix.com/title/81254224.
3. Brené Brown, "Listening to Shame."

CHAPTER 7: 50 SHADES OF *THEY*

1. Jia Jiang, *Rejection Proof: How I Beat Fear and Became Invincible Through 100 Days of Rejection* (New York: Crown Publishing, 2015).
2. Jia Jiang, "What I Learned from 100 Days of Rejection," TED Talk, December 2016, https://www.ted.com/talks /jia_jiang_what_I_learned_from_100_days_of_rejection.

CHAPTER 8: ALL I DO IS WIN

1. Octavia Butler, *Bloodchild and Other Stories* (New York: Seven Stories Press, 2005), 141.
2. Jack Dorsey (interview), "Jack Dorsey on Working for Two Companies Full-Time," Techonomy Media (Techonomy Editorial Events), August 27, 2012, https:// techonomy.com/2012/08/video-jack-dorsey-on-working -for-two-companies-full-time/.

CHAPTER 9: FRIENDS, DON'T FAIL ME NOW

1. "12 Step Programs for Drug Rehab and Alcohol Treatment," American Addiction Centers, updated January 11, 2021, https://americanaddictioncenters.org /rehab-guide/12-step.
2. Stacey Hanke, "Three Steps to Overcoming Resistance,"

Forbes, August 14, 2018, https://www.forbes.com/sites
/forbescoachescouncil/2018/08/14/three-steps-to
-overcoming-resistance/?sh=4bc9c5985eae.

3. Wayne Baker, quoted in Adam Grant, *Give and Take:
Why Helping Others Drives Our Success* (New York: Penguin
Books, 2014), 34.

4. Edgar H. Schein, *Organizational Culture and Leadership*
(Hoboken, NJ: John Wiley & Sons, 2016), 190.

CHAPTER 10: JUST DO IT SCARED

1. Sara Blakely, LinkedIn, August 2020, https://www
.linkedin.com/posts/sarablakely27_entrepreneur
-business-spanx-activity-6693519249580945408-rG4k/.

CHAPTER 11: IF AT FIRST YOU DON'T FAIL, TRY AGAIN

1. Danielle Douglas, "Blockbuster May Cut More Locations
as Part of Bankruptcy," *Washington Post*, October 10,
2010, https://www.washingtonpost.com/wp-dyn
/content/article/2010/10/10/AR2010101003147.html.

2. Marc Graser, "Epic Fail: How Blockbuster Could Have
Owned Netflix," *Variety*, November 12, 2013,
https://variety.com/2013/biz/news/epic-fail-how
-blockbuster-could-have-owned-netflix-1200823443/.

3. Ariel Shapiro, "Netflix Stock Hits Record High, Is
Now Worth More Than Disney," *Forbes*, April 16, 2020,
https://www.forbes.com/sites/arielshapiro/2020/04/16
/netflix-stock-hits-record-high-is-now-worth-more-
than-disney/.

4. "Population Projections," United States Census Bureau,
March 13, 2018, revised September 6, 2018 and
October 8, 2019, https://www.census.gov/newsroom
/press-kits/2018/pop-projections.html.

5. Anita Elberse and Stacie Smith, "Beyoncé," Harvard Business School Case 515-036, August 2014 (revised October 2014).

6. Elberse and Smith, "Beyoncé."

7. Bob Iger, "Bob Iger Teaches Business Strategy and Leadership," Master Class, https://www.masterclass.com/classes/bob-iger-teaches-business-strategy-and-leadership.

8. Sarah Whitten, "14 Years, 4 Acquisitions, 1 Bob Iger: How Disney's CEO Revitalized an Iconic American Brand," CNBC, August 6, 2019, https://https://www.cnbc.com/2019/08/06/bob-iger-forever-changed-disney-with-4-key-acquisitions.html.

9. Walter Loeb, "Amazon Is the Biggest Investor in the Future, Spends $22.6 Billion on R&D," Forbes, November 1, 2018, https://www.forbes.com/sites/walterloeb/2018/11/01/amazon-is-biggest-investor-for-the-future/.

10. Scott Mautz, "Jeff Bezos Just Released His Annual Shareholder Letter and Said 1 Counterintuitive Thing Is the Key to Continued Business Growth," Inc., April 12, 2019, https://www.inc.com/scott-mautz/jeff-bezos-just-released-his-annual-shareholder-letter-said-1-counterintuitive-thing-is-key-to-continued-business-growth.html.

11. Todd Haselton, "Here's Jeff Bezos' Annual Shareholder Letter," CNBC, April 11, 2019, https://www.cnbc.com/2019/04/11/jeff-bezos-annual-shareholder-letter.html.

CHAPTER 12: DON'T WAIT FOR MONDAY

1. Erwin Raphael McManus, The Last Arrow: Save Nothing for the Next Life (Colorado Springs, CO: WaterBrook, 2017), 107.

ABOUT THE AUTHOR

Ryan Leak is an author, speaker, executive coach, and filmmaker. He's known for two documentaries: *The Surprise Wedding* and *Chasing Failure*. The son of a preacher man, Ryan grew up in the church with a marketplace passion. Today, Ryan splits his time between speaking in churches and doing executive coaching and speaking in corporate America through his company The Ryan Leak Group, LLC.

Ryan has a unique church position in that he is on the teaching team of five megachurches. He rotates speaking at each of them seven to eight times a year. He regularly teaches 48,000 people between those five churches. Ryan does about 120 events each year, reaching 200,000 people, and trains approximately 15,000 leaders.

Ryan and his wife, Amanda, reside in Dallas, Texas, with their two children, Jaxson and Roman.

FOR CONTINUED SUPPORT AND MOTIVATION AS YOU CHASE FAILURE, RYAN LEAK IS THERE FOR YOU.

Follow him on social media: @ryanleak, tune into his podcasts, subscribe for inspirational content, and book Ryan for speaking engagements at his website.